T0330395

The Economics of Open Access

NEW HORIZONS IN LAW AND ECONOMICS

Series Editors: Gerrit De Geest, *Washington University in St. Louis, USA*, Roger Van den Bergh, *Erasmus University Rotterdam, The Netherlands* and Thomas S. Ulen, *University of Illinois at Urbana-Champaign, USA*

The application of economic ideas and theories to the law and the explanation of markets and public economics from a legal point of view is recognized as one of the most exciting developments in both economics and the law. This important series is designed to make a significant contribution to the development of law and economics.

The main emphasis is on the development and application of new ideas. The series provides a forum for original research in areas such as criminal law, civil law, labour law, corporate law, family law, regulation and privatization, tax, risk and insurance and competition law. International in its approach it includes some of the best theoretical and empirical work from both well-established researchers and the new generation of scholars.

Titles in the series include:

The Economics of Open Access

On the Future of Academic Publishing

Thomas Eger

Professor Emeritus of Law and Economics, University of Hamburg, Germany

Marc Scheufen

Senior Research Fellow, Law Faculty, Ruhr University of Bochum, Germany

NEW HORIZONS IN LAW AND ECONOMICS

Cheltenham, UK • Northampton, MA, USA

Published by
Edward Elgar Publishing Limited
The Lypiatts
15 Lansdown Road
Cheltenham
Glos GL50 2JA
UK

Edward Elgar Publishing, Inc.
William Pratt House
9 Dewey Court
Northampton
Massachusetts 01060
USA

A catalogue record for this book
is available from the British Library

Library of Congress Control Number: 2018931652

This book is available electronically in the **Elgar**online
Law subject collection
DOI 10.4337/9781785365768

ISBN 978 1 78536 575 1 (cased)
ISBN 978 1 78536 576 8 (eBook)

Typeset by Servis Filmsetting Ltd, Stockport, Cheshire
Printed on FSC approved paper
Printed and bound in Great Britain by Marston Book Services Ltd, Oxfordshire

Contents

Acknowledgments

The authors of this book are grateful to the many people who have made this project possible. Since a large part of the book is based on the international online survey we conducted between 2012 and 2015, we wish to thank all those who contributed to the success of the survey. This includes Simon Gattmann, Henning Grell, Ann-Katrin Hengevoß and André Plaster for technical support, Andreas Knobelsdorf, who familiarised us with serial price statistics, as well as Ivo Gico Jr. from the Universidade Católica de Brasília, Abdel-Hameed Nawar from the University of Cairo, P. G. Babu from the Indira Gandhi Institute of Development Research in Mumbai, Guido Westkamp from Queen Mary University of London, and Giancarlo F. Frosio from Stanford Law School for facilitating cooperation with the individual countries. Moreover, many people helped us translate the questionnaires into the languages of the countries covered by the survey and to gather essential contact data: Ella Azerad, Meltem Bayramli, Amélie van Belleghem, Julia Bodnarova, Audra Bohlen, Anne Sofie Brusendorff, Robin Burkill, Emanuela Carbonara, Elisabete Castro, Maria Cecilia Dómine, Niva Elkin-Koren, Elif Erdemoglu, Daniela Garcia Ferreira, Martin Fiala, Carolin Frey, Ariane Garciabueno, Galya Georgieva, Bart van Heeswijk, Nie Hua, Malin Hüttmann, Eglé Jonyke, Mate Kakas, Angeliki Karakoliou, Vaia Karapanou, Zara Kaushik, Klara Keglevic, Min Lin, Ann MacManus, Ilari Määttä, Jurate Misonyte, Irina Nikiforova, Iris de Orte, Konstantinos Pilpilidis, Alan Ralph, Taina Rintala, Mariam Saleh, Yun Schüler-Zhou, Margot Schüller, Mostafa Serour, Agnes Strauß and Damian Zajackowski.

We also wish to thank Daniel Meierrieks, our co-author for the evaluations of the surveys on a subset of the countries, as well as Jerg Gutmann, Manfred Kraft, Stefan Voigt and many scholars from several Law and Economics Associations in Europe, Asia and the Middle East for valuable comments. Special thanks go to Sönke Häseler, who not only commented extensively on earlier drafts but also provided meticulous proofreading. We also wish to thank Niklas Jochheim for his support in completing and formatting the bibliography and the index. Finally, we are truly grateful for the excellent cooperation with the staff at Edward Elgar Publishing, whose assistance with the publication of this book was invaluable.

Abbreviations

AGORA	Access to Global Online Research in Agriculture
Agri	Agriculture and Forestry
ANR	Agence Nationale de la Recherche
APC	Article-Processing Charges
ARDI	Access to Research for Development and Innovation
Bio	Biology and Life Science
Bus	Business and Economics
CA	Closed Access
CC	Creative Commons
CC-BY	Creative Commons Attribution License
CC-NC	Creative Commons Non-Commercial License
CC-ND	Creative Commons No Derivatives License
CC-SA	Creative Commons Share Alike
CERN	Conseil Européen pour la Recherche Nucléaire
Chem	Chemistry
CNRS	Centre National de la Recherche Scientifique
COAR	Confederation of Open Access Repositories
DOAJ	Directory of Open Access Journals
DOAR	Directory of Open Access Repositories
Earth	Earth and Environmental Science
EU	European Union
EUR	Euro (€)
FASTR	Fair Access to Science and Technology Act
FiveIF	Five year Impact Factor
FP7	Seventh Framework Program
FRPAA	Federal Research Public Access Act
GBP	Great Britain Pound
GPL	General Public License
HAL	Hyper Articles en Ligne
Health	Health Science
HEFCE	Higher Education Funding Council for England
HINARI	Health Internetwork Access to Research Initiative
Hist	History and Archaeology
IF	(Two year) Impact Factor

IV	Instrumental Variables
JCR	Journal Citation Report
LaPo	Law and Political Science
Lang	Language and Linguistics
LISU	Library and Information Science Unit
Math	Mathematics and Statistics
MedOANet	Mediterranean Open Access Network
MDPI	Multidisciplinary Publishing Institute
NIH	National Institutes of Health
OA	Open Access
ORD	Open Research Data
OARE	Online Access to Research in the Environment
OLS	Ordinary Least Squares
Phys	Physics and Astronomy
PLOS	Public Library of Science
PMC	PubMed Central
RePEc	Research Papers in Economics
ROAR	Registry of Open Access Repositories
ROARMAP	Registry of Open Access Repositories Mandates and Policies
ScieELO	Scientific Electronic Library Online
SCI	Science Citation Index
SCOAP	Sponsoring Consortium for Open Access Publishing in Particle Physics
SMT	Science Mathematics Technology
Social	Social Science
SSCI	Social Science Citation Index
SSRN	Social Science Research Network
Tech	Technology and Engineering
UK	United Kingdom
UNESCO	United Nations Educational, Scientific and Cultural Organization
US	United States
WHO	World Health Organisation
WoS	Web of Science

1. Introduction

1.1 DEVELOPMENT OF THE ACADEMIC PUBLISHING MARKET AND THE SERIALS CRISIS

In most disciplines, scholarly journals have become the central medium of academic communication. Any academic library that aims to provide its users with the relevant research results of the international academic community and thereby to foster its reputation must invest considerable amounts to maintain an up-to-date stock of scholarly journals. The number of scholarly journals and the number of articles published each year have grown steadily. In 2014, about 28,100 active peer-reviewed English-language journals were available, plus another 6,450 journals in other languages, containing a total of about 2.5 million articles per year (STM Report 2015: 6). The largest share of these research papers originates from the US (about 23 percent of the global output), 17 percent are from China, which has experienced a dramatic growth in research output over the last 15 years, 7 percent from the UK, 6 percent each from Germany and Japan, and 4 percent from France (ibid.: 7).

Over the last 40 years, the market for scholarly journals has experienced a number of dramatic changes:

- Not least since the mass expansion of academic education not only in the Anglo-Saxon countries after World War II and the increasing size of faculty, publications in peer-reviewed, highly ranked journals have become an important precondition for academic careers in many disciplines.[1]
- Since then, the hitherto dominant publishers of such material – non-for-profit organizations, such as learned societies and universities – have increasingly ceded market shares to commercial publishers.
- Today's market for scholarly journals is characterized by a high degree of concentration. The five major commercial publishers – Elsevier,

---

[1] See e.g. Willinsky (2009: 13–37).

Springer, Wiley, Taylor & Francis and SAGE – already cover more than half of the market for scholarly journals.[2] Since most journals, even within the same discipline, are not close substitutes but differ considerably with respect to their reputation with authors and readers, each journal constitutes a kind of 'mini-monopoly'.[3]

- With the development of digitization and the advent of the internet, an increasing share of scholarly journals have become available electronically, some exclusively, some in addition to the print versions. Few journals remain available in print version only.[4]
- In particular, the 'big five' commercial publishers have increasingly replaced the traditional model of offering subscriptions to individual journals by so-called 'big deals', i.e. they sell bundles of content (print copies and licenses to access electronic journals) to (consortia of) academic libraries (Suber 2012: 32–33). Holding a sufficiently large portfolio of strong, highly ranked journals, this bundling enables publishers to urge libraries to subscribe also to less important journals, which further increases the publishers' profits.

All of these developments have led to an enormous increase in journal prices over the last 30 years, placing substantial pressure on academic library budgets.[5] Facing sharply increasing serial unit cost and serial expenditures, libraries have had to allocate an increasing share of their budgets to scholarly journals, to the detriment of expenditures on monographs, which have stagnated. While the North-American research libraries spent about a third more on journals than on monographs in 1987, this ratio had risen to about four to one by 2011. This stagnation of

---

[2]   Larivière et al. (2015).

[3]   '. . . high subscription fees and excess publisher profits are due mostly to the monopoly nature of each individual article, not to some more aggregated measure of concentration in the journal market' (Armstrong 2015: F11). See also Suber (2012: 39).

[4]   According to Prabha (2007), who collected data on 515 journals subscribed to by member libraries of the Association of Research Libraries, a non-for-profit organization of the leading research libraries in the US and Canada, within only four years (2002–06), the share of journals that are only available in print version dropped dramatically from 64 percent to 31 percent, while the share of journals only available in electronic version increased from 5 percent to 37 percent, and the share of journals available in both formats increased from 31 percent to 33 percent. Other studies, quoted in the STM report 2015, place the share of online-availability of scholarly journals in 2008 at 96 percent for Science, Technology and Medicine, and 87 percent for Arts, Humanities and Social Sciences.

[5]   See also Ramello (2010).

monograph expenditure was felt in particular by the humanities, in which these types of publication are especially important.

1.2 COPYRIGHT PROTECTION IN ACADEMIC PUBLISHING

So far, the commercial publishers' business success has strongly depended on copyright protection. Copyright law covers works of literature, science and art, in other words the creation of specific information such as texts or sheet music. An essential property of that information is its lack of rivalry in consumption. One man's enjoyment of a text or song does not interfere with anyone else's desire to read the same text or listen to the same song. Nobel laureate Paul A. Samuelson introduced the term 'collective consumption goods' for such goods and he developed conditions for their optimal supply (Samuelson 1954).[6] By contrast, one person's use of a private consumption good, such as food, clothing or mobile phones, prejudices everyone else's use, so we have rivalry in consumption.

How, then, can we reconcile the non-rivalry of works of literature, science or art with exclusive property rights? This question is easily posed but much harder to answer. On the one hand, as soon as a work becomes a 'collective consumption good' and its use is non-rivalrous, the exclusion of interested parties from its use is almost impossible to justify on economic grounds. Every additional consumer draws a benefit from using the work without reducing the welfare of others. Hence, the admission of additional users constitutes a Pareto improvement; a restriction of access would imply a loss of welfare. At the same time, it must be noted that not only end-users consume the work. The creator herself will have been inspired to some extent by other existing works. With strong copyright, such inspiration

---

[6]   Some authors in this context speak of 'public goods', which are characterized by non-rivalry in consumption and the non-excludability of non-payers. This definition is due to Musgrave, who sought an economic rationale for the fact that goods such as a country's internal and external security are not supplied by the market but instead by the state, and that they are financed through compulsory levies. Like other rights to immaterial goods, however, copyright accomplishes exactly that excludability. Accordingly, Landes and Posner (2003: 14) remark on the concept of a public good: 'It sounds like a good produced by the government as opposed to the private sector. That is true of public goods that people cannot be excluded from having the benefit of even if they don't contribute to the cost of supplying the goods. The clearest example is national defense. Many public goods, however, including intellectual property, are excludable in the sense that it is possible to condition access to them on payment.'

would be less available, so the cost of creating new works would increase. On the other hand, works of literature, science and art are not created out of thin air; their production requires time, creativity and money. These are scarce resources, and creative individuals will only be prepared to invest in the creation of new works if the investment promises an adequate return.

In brief, copyright law is a method to induce the creation and dissemination of new information by restricting access to existing information. From an economic perspective, the debate on copyright in general, and on copyright in the age of digitization and the internet in particular, should thus focus on the optimal design of copyright rules: Sufficiently strong incentives should be established for the creation of works of literature, science and art, while at the same time society should not be burdened with unnecessarily high costs. The essential issue concerns the trade-off between underproduction of information, i.e. works of literature, science and art caused by insufficient protection of the creator, and the underuse of this information caused by overly strict exclusive property rights for the creator.

How are academic authors special? As Suber (2012: 129–30) correctly states, the conventional wisdom that authors need copyright to give them an incentive to write does not hold for authors of research articles – and this for two reasons: On the one hand, authors who submit articles to scholarly journals are not interested in royalties for these articles and they are usually not paid by the journal. Rather, they are interested in readership, citations and impact in order to increase their reputation.[7] On the other hand, scholarly authors typically transfer their copyrights exclusively to the publisher, to enable him to cover the cost of providing a number of valuable services, including (Armstrong 2015: F3):

- preparing the definite typeset version of an article,
- certifying an article's quality via the journal's reputation for selectivity,
- improving the original manuscript with suggestions from reviewers and editors, and
- distributing the published article to those (and only those) permitted to read it.

The crucial question is to what extent the publisher contributes to the value added of the creation and dissemination of research articles compared to the other participants, such as authors, editors and reviewers,

---

[7]   See also Shavell (2010: 10): '. . .the utility of academic authors is increased by the readership of their published works because they gain esteem from readership.'

who are typically paid by their universities (Suber 2012: 37), and to what extent publishers of research articles must be protected by copyright law to give them an incentive to provide the required services at reasonable cost. Digitization and the advent of the internet have at the same time dramatically lowered some publishing costs and also increased the journals' ability to generate revenues (for some details see Armstrong 2015: F9).

Let us examine the cost side first. The availability of word processing software has certainly reduced the journals' typesetting cost. Moreover, editorial software reduces the cost of managing the submission and peer-review process. Less clear is the impact of the internet on the second type of publisher's services, the certification of the quality of an article. An academic article is an experience good. Time and effort are required to read an article and to 'experience' its quality.[8] The fact that an article is published by a highly reputed journal following an intensive review process provides valuable ex ante quality information to the reader. At the same time, authors will benefit from this quality signal to the extent that their reputation and career depend on publications in highly ranked journals. The internet may reduce the benefit of quality certification by journals in the future as citation and download data for individual articles (e.g. via Google Scholar) and even comments on individual papers are becoming available. The net benefit of the third function of traditional journals – improving the manuscript by suggestions from reviewers and editors – is ambiguous. On the one hand, both authors and readers benefit from improved quality. On the other hand, this benefit comes at a cost, since authors must spend time and effort to cope with the reviewers' sometimes conflicting recommendations and readers have to wait a long time for a submitted paper to be published. Finally, the dissemination of the articles via the internet occurs at zero marginal cost.

However, not only have the costs of the publishers' services declined, but their ability to create revenues has indeed increased. Thanks to the electronic dissemination of the articles, publishers can monitor download activity and fine-tune their prices accordingly (Armstrong 2015: F9). Moreover, copyright protection enables publishers to restrict access to electronic journals in a way 'that leaves users with fewer rights than they had with print journals', adding 'a permission crisis on top of the pricing crisis' (Suber 2012: 34).

Thus, the advent of modern software and the internet has, on the one hand, reduced the cost of producing, selecting, editing and disseminating

---

[8] Nelson (1970) contrasted experience goods with search goods, where only the latter's quality can easily be observed before purchase.

research articles. On the other hand, the existing copyright law enables publishers to restrict access to these electronic articles far beyond what is possible in the case of print editions. Therefore, it comes as no surprise that the advent of the internet has triggered critical discussions about the role of copyright law under these new conditions.[9] The discussion already began in the 1980s, when Richard M. Stallman, a software developer at the MIT, criticized the restricted access to computer operating systems. In 1989, he devised a new type of license, the GNU Public License (GPL), which is completely different from traditional software licenses, applying an alternative approach to the use of copyright without denying the original creator's copyright protection. Instead of using the copyright protection of software to restrict the end-user's freedom to modify the underlying source code and/or to redistribute the program, Stallman made access to the source code public and allowed the users to view, redistribute and, most importantly, modify the program, where any modification to the software must be redistributed on the same terms (Eve, 2014: 17).[10] Based on this principle, Harvard legal scholar Lawrence Lessig in 2001 founded the non-for-profit organization 'Creative Commons', which offers a set of licenses that 'are designed to allow others to redistribute, modify, translate and computationally analyze works', with different levels of permissiveness (Eve 2014: 20).

1.3 THE ORIGINS OF OPEN ACCESS IN ACADEMIC PUBLISHING

The development of digitization, the advent of the internet and the discontent with the existing price barriers and technical barriers to the access to research articles induced many scholars, initially in the US, to support open access to these articles. Several initiatives sought either of two roads to open access: (1) *gold open access*, i.e. the establishment of electronic journals with open access for all readers, often based on creative common licenses; the journals' costs are covered not by submission fees but from other sources, such as authors' fees or subsidies from learned societies or research sponsors; and (2) *green open access*, i.e. the establishment of so-called open access repositories that enable scholarly authors to upload (or self-archive) their papers, either independently of, prior to, or after publication in traditional journals.

---

[9]   See, for example, the discussion in Eve (2014: 16–21).
[10] As a wordplay, Stallman coined the concept of 'copyleft'.

An early active promoter of open access in the US was cognitive scientist Stevan Harnad. Already in 1989, he launched the free online journal *Psycoloquy* and later supported the self-archiving of research articles. In the Overture to his 'Subversive Proposal' (1994) he stated:

> For centuries, it was only out of reluctant necessity that authors of esoteric publications made the Faustian bargain to allow a price-tag to be erected as a barrier between their work and its (tiny) intended readership because that was the only way to make their work public in the era when paper publication (and its substantial real expenses) were the only way to do so.[11]

In 1997, he launched the repository 'cogprints', which specializes in psychology, neuroscience, linguistics and computer science. Already in 1991, physicist Paul Ginsparg had established arXiv, an open access repository for papers in physics, mathematics, computer science, quantitative biology, quantitative finance and statistics, and in 1994, Wayne Marr and Michael Jensen launched another important open access repository, the 'social science research network' (SSRN), which was acquired by Elsevier in 2016. In the last decade of the 20th century, more open access journals and repositories were launched in particular in the US, and many universities established open digital archives.

The evolution of open access subsequently spread beyond the US. The most impressive example is the establishment of SciELO ('Scientific Electronic Library Online'), which was established in 1997 in Brazil and today covers most Latin American countries, South Africa, Spain and Portugal. Another example is the Hindawi Publishing Corporation, which was founded in Cairo in 1997. Originally established as a traditional publisher of academic journals, Hindawi soon began to publish selected journals in open access mode and eventually dropped publication based on subscription fees altogether in 2007. As of 2016, their portfolio comprises more than 400 peer-reviewed academic journals. Finally, Medknow Publications, founded in 1997 in Mumbai, specializes in scholarly journals in medicine and natural science. At the turn of the millennium, Medknow converted most of their journals to open access. They were acquired by Wolters Kluwer Health in 2011 and, as of 2016, have 372 journals in their portfolio.

In the early 2000s, academic scholars, representatives of research libraries and research sponsors from all over the world launched several initiatives to foster open access to scholarly articles, including

---

[11] Available at https://groups.google.com/forum/?hl=en#!topic/bit.listserv.vpie j-l/BoKENhK0_00.

the 'Budapest Open Access Initiative'[12] (February 2002), the 'Bethesda Statement on Open Access Publishing'[13] (June 2003), and the 'Berlin Declaration on Open Access to Knowledge in the Sciences and Humanities'[14] (October 2003).

The Budapest Open Access Initiative defines open access as follows:[15]

> By 'open access' to this literature, we mean its free availability on the public internet, permitting any users to read, download, copy, distribute, print, search, or link to the full texts of these articles, crawl them for indexing, pass them as data to software, or use them for any other lawful purpose, without financial, legal, or technical barriers other than those inseparable from gaining access to the internet itself. The only constraint on reproduction and distribution, and the only role for copyright in this domain, should be to give authors control over the integrity of their work and the right to be properly acknowledged and cited.

The Berlin Declaration contains the following, almost identical condensed form (which is also very similar to the formulation in the Bethesda Statement):

> The author(s) and right holder(s) of such contributions grant(s) to all users a free, irrevocable, worldwide, (perpetual) right of access to, and a license to copy, use, distribute, transmit and display the work publicly and to make and distribute derivative works, in any digital medium for any responsible purpose, subject to proper attribution of authorship.

These statements and declarations triggered a boom of open access activities, also in Europe. Manifold bottom-up initiatives by academic libraries, research sponsors and individual activists developed, research sponsors supported gold and/or green access by open access mandates, and in some countries, open access was even promoted by new legislation. These initiatives and policies will be the subject of our more detailed discussions throughout this book.

In the following, we start with an extensive presentation of how the academic publishing market has developed over time (chapter 2). In this chapter, we not only discuss the specific reward structure faced by authors of scholarly articles in different disciplines but we also explore

---

[12] www.soros.org/openaccess/read.
[13] www.earlham.edu/~peters/fos/bethesda.htm.
[14] https://openaccess.mpg.de/Berlin-Declaration.
[15] The principal drafter was Peter Suber, currently the Director of the Office for Scholarly Communication at Harvard University and a very active supporter of open access.

important features of the supply and the demand side of the scholarly journals publishing market. Moreover, we elaborate on the development of gold and green open access (OA) and their political support in selected countries. Having discussed important *objective data* on OA, in chapter 3 we evaluate the results of an international survey we conducted between 2012 and 2015 in 25 countries. This chapter provides some insights on the experiences of scholarly authors with and their attitudes towards OA, and complements chapter 2 by providing the corresponding *subjective data*. Based on these results, chapter 4 analyzes the reasons for the success (or lack thereof) of recent policy attempts to foster OA in academic publishing. Chapter 5 summarizes the most important results and concludes with some more general insights regarding the future of academic publishing. The appendix (chapter 6) provides some additional information on the tables and figures used in the text.

2. The academic publishing market

2.1 THE ECONOMICS OF ACADEMIC PUBLISHING

To understand the organization of academic publishing, we need to be familiar with the motivational forces of individual researchers to publish academic works, as well as with the market conditions and structural constraints of the academic publishing market. We will start by examining the reward structure, asking what motivates scholars to write academic articles. Next, we will address the publishing market, pointing out the different options for researchers to publish their works and showing, towards the end of the chapter, why some of these options are more attractive to researchers in certain disciplines than in others. From this we will derive characteristics of several publishing cultures that summarily determine researchers' attitudes towards the open access (OA) versus the traditional closed access (CA) mode of publishing.[1]

2.1.1 The Reward Structure in Science

Why do academic authors publish articles in scholarly journals? To see this, we need to question researchers' motives to publish their work more generally. Motivation can usefully be distinguished into the *intrinsic* and the *extrinsic* types.[2] 'Intrinsic motivation is defined as the doing of an activity for its inherent satisfactions rather than for some separable consequence. When intrinsically motivated, a person is moved to act for the fun or challenge entailed rather than because of external prods, pressures, or rewards' (Ryan and Deci 2000: 56). For academic authors, a typical intrinsic motive is 'curiosity': They derive utility directly from 'understanding the world' or, more precisely, from solving a research question. However, this motive is not sufficient to explain why researchers want to *publish*

---

[1] We will elaborate further on the determinants of OA publishing when discussing our international survey results in chapter 3.

[2] See, for example, from a psychologist's point of view, Ryan and Deci (2000). For economists, see in particular the book by Frey (1997, especially chapter 3) and for a more specific application Bénabou and Tirole (2003).

their research results. In general, most activities in life are extrinsically motivated: '*Extrinsic motivation* is a construct that pertains whenever an activity is done in order to attain some separable outcome' (Ryan and Deci 2000: 60). That outcome may be monetary rewards or (the avoidance of) monetary punishment, but equally non-monetary rewards, such as social esteem and recognition, and the avoidance of non-monetary punishments, such as losing reputation and being imprisoned. To scholarly authors, the most important (extrinsic) motive to publish their works is the recognition of priority of their research and the expected gain in reputation with their peers. As a matter of fact, in most academic disciplines, direct monetary rewards for published articles do not play any role, whereas the researchers' salaries to some extent depend on their reputation in the long run. While the distinction between intrinsic and extrinsic motivation is generally considered meaningful, it remains controversial where exactly to draw the line between the two types of motivation and under what conditions extrinsic motivation supports or undermines intrinsic motivation. With respect to academic authors, there is a discussion as to what extent a strengthening of an outcome-based reward system negatively affects the curiosity element of research (see more on this in chapter 4).

Anyway, in practice, researchers accumulate reputational capital over their scientific careers, signalling their contributions to the advancement of science. Each publication of high quality adds reputation to the researcher's CV.[3] Importantly, what matters for a researcher's image with the scientific community is not the number but the quality of academic works. In most fields of research, quality is proxied by measures of impact, such as the impact factor compiled in the Journal Citation Reports. The more frequently the articles within a particular journal are cited, the higher the journal's impact factor. Thus, to compare publication records, researchers' publications are often weighted by the impact factors of the journals they have appeared in. Though not equally applicable to all academic disciplines, this is certainly true for the natural sciences and economics, and to some extent also for the social sciences. We will see that this academic reward structure has a strong impact on the attractiveness of OA publishing.

---

[3] On the more general economics of science literature see especially Merton (1957, 1973), Dasgupta and David (1987), as well as Stephan and Levin (1992). For a literature review on the economics of science see Coccia (2006).

2.1.2   The Organization of Academic Publishing

Scientific journals have been an important forum for scholarly communication for hundreds of years.[4] The first scientific journal, the *Journal des Sçavans*, was published in Paris on 5 January 1665. After the French Revolution, it reappeared in 1797 under the new title *Journal des Savants*, served as a model for a number of scholarly journals in Europe during the 17th and 18th centuries, and today continues to be a leading journal in the Humanities. A few months later, on 6 March 1665, Henry Oldenburg, the first secretary of the Royal Society of London, edited a second scholarly journal, the *Philosophical Transactions*, with a focus on science. This journal introduced the peer-review process, was home to the priority disputes between Newton and Leibniz, and still exists today. More specialized journals appeared in the 18th and 19th centuries, most of which were published by learned societies. Only at the end of the 19th century did university presses gain importance as publishers of scholarly journals.

Today, in most disciplines, particularly in science, technology and medicine, but also in the social sciences and economics, research articles published in peer-reviewed scholarly journals are the pivotal means of scholarly communication. In other disciplines, in particular the humanities, the publication of research results in books, i.e. monographs, conference volumes and so on, still retains great importance.[5]

While traditionally most scholarly journals were published by non-profit organizations such as learned societies and universities, since World War II, a growing number of journals have been published by commercial publishers. All publishers relied on the 'subscription model', charging the readers a fee for their subscription to the journal. Subscribers are typically university libraries or libraries of faculties and research institutes, but also individual scholars, in particular if they are members of learned societies, whose membership fees often include subscription fees to their journals. This business model continues to exist in the age of electronic academic publishing. Most journals are now available electronically via the internet, some in addition to the print version, while a dwindling share remains available in print version only. Academic libraries acquire licenses to allow scholars and students to access these journals via the internet. Since the libraries pay for the licenses, these journals are called *toll access* journals (Suber 2012: 6). With the advent of electronic publishing since the 1990s,

---

[4]   On the following, see Regazzi (2015: 22–33).
[5]   On the history of the scholarly book since 1548, see for example Regazzi (2015: 47–76).

the big commercial publishers, which own hundreds of journals from all disciplines, began to offer the academic libraries (or consortia of libraries) so called 'Big Deals'. In such a multi-year contract for bundled site licenses between the publisher and the library, the latter agrees to subscribe to its existing base of print subscriptions at an annually increasing price; in exchange, the publisher grants the library access to an electronic journal database at a substantial discount.[6] The bundle prices vary dramatically from institution to institution, and publishers urge the libraries to keep the prices confidential (Bergstrom et al. 2014). Individual readers who have no access to an academic library with the required licenses may pay for access to individual electronic articles in toll access journals. Baldwin (2014: 366) describes the commercial academic publishers' business model very clearly: 'Their business model was a marvel: sell scholarship back to the same universities whose scientists had produced, written, peer reviewed, and edited it largely for free. Profit margins of between 35 per cent and 40 per cent were the happy outcome.'[7]

While there are many ways to grant open access to research articles, the current discussion distinguishes between two such ways: the gold road and the green road.[8] The *gold road* refers to open access journals that, like the traditional toll access journals, are mostly peer-reviewed (see Table 2.8). However, since anyone with a computer and access to the internet can (at least) read the journal articles without paying, the traditional subscription model ceases to work with open access. Thus, alternative business models are required for the publishers to cover their costs. One option is to demand so-called article-processing charges (APC) from the authors or their sponsors. In addition to or instead of APCs, most OA publishers draw on other sources of income, including grants (e.g. the Public Library of Science), print subscriptions (e.g. Hindawi Publishing Corporation) or advertising (e.g. Medknow Publications).

In contrast to traditional toll access journals, all open access journals have removed the price barriers to access. However, some permission barriers protected by copyright law typically remain. Suber (2012: 65) therefore distinguishes between *gratis open access* (only price barriers are removed) and *libre open access* (price barriers and at least some permission barriers are removed). About 20 percent of the open access journals listed in the Directory of Open Access Journals (DOAJ) remove some permission barriers by relying on various types of licenses between authors and

---

[6] For more details, see Edlin and Rubinfeld (2004 and 2005).
[7] For more details, see Ramello (2010) and Larivière et al (2015: 5).
[8] See Harnad et al. (2004).

publishers that are designed by the non-for-profit organization 'Creative Commons (CC)'.[9] This organization offers a number of licenses with different degrees of permission barriers. Apart from the public domain (CC-Zero), the least restrictive license is the CC-BY license, which permits any use so long as the work remains attributed to the original author. Other CC-licenses are more restrictive, such as the CC-BY-NC license (attribution required, commercial use banned), the CC-BY-ND license (attribution required, commercial use permitted, derivative works banned), or the CC-BY-SA license (attribution required, commercial use permitted, derivative works must be shared under the same licensing terms).[10] Less than 11 percent of the titles in the DOAJ use the CC-BY license, and 80 percent do not use any kind of CC license, most of which operate under full copyright, with permission constrained to the 'fair use' exemptions (Suber 2012: 72). Some publishers offer *hybrid open access journals*,[11] where readers generally have to pay for access to the articles unless the author has paid an APC for a specific article. Springer for example uses this model under the term 'Open Choice', which allows authors to publish open access in most of Springer's subscription-based journals. However, some critics have denounced this business model as 'double dipping', accusing the publisher of collecting money twice, 'once when subscriptions are paid by the universities and research organizations and once when authors are additionally charged open access fees' (Mittermaier 2015: 3–4). The reason is that there is some doubt as to whether an increase in the number of open access articles actually leads to a corresponding decrease in the subscription fee of a journal. Nobody really knows the counterfactual, i.e. the subscription fee the journal would charge without any open access articles (Bergstrom and Rubinfeld 2010: 145).

The *green road* by contrast refers to open access repositories, i.e. online collections of research papers and other documents.[12] Important in this context are pre-prints and post-prints of articles (to be) published in toll access journals. Unlike open access journals, the repositories do not

---

[9] https://creativecommons.org.
[10] For more details, see Scheufen (2015: 67).
[11]   The lack of a register of hybrid OA journals makes it difficult to find reliable data on the importance of hybrid OA. Recently, Laakso and Björk (2016) conducted a bottom-up study on the importance of hybrid OA with the five largest publishers of scholarly journals (Elsevier, Springer, Wiley-Blackwell, Taylor & Francis, and Sage). They found that the number of articles published as hybrid OA increased from 666 articles in 2007 to 13,994 articles in 2013. For journals with at least one hybrid OA article, the share of hybrid articles among all articles published from 2011 to 2013 was 3.8 percent.
[12] For the following, see e.g. Suber 2012: 52 ff.

perform their own peer review but restrict themselves to brief plausibility or quality checks. However, repositories do host many articles that have been peer-reviewed elsewhere. Another difference concerns the allocation of copyright. An author who publishes in an open access journal typically transfers the necessary rights and permissions to the publisher. When authors deposit articles in repositories, in most cases they will already have transferred copyright to the publisher of a toll access journal.

A distinction should be made between *subject-based (disciplinary) repositories*, such as SSRN for the social sciences and arXiv for physics and some neighboring disciplines, and *institutional repositories* administered by universities, faculties or research institutes. Repositories generally grant *gratis open access*, but as with open access journals, they also feature more or less strict permission barriers (different degrees of *libre open access*). Though most disciplinary and institutional repositories respect the authors' or publishers' copyrights, some do not. Since those repositories that do not respect publishers' copyrights aim to provide access for less privileged institutions and countries, their service is sometimes referred to as *Robin Hood open access* (Archambault et al. 2014: 4). The most prominent example is Sci-Hub, an online repository that was founded in 2011 by a young scholar from Kazakhstan and comprises over 60 million scholarly articles as of 2017. Following complaints from Elsevier, Sci-Hub has switched domains several times.[13] More recently, the disciplinary and institutional repositories have been complemented by *academic social networks*, such as Research Gate, Mendeley and Academia.

2.2   THE ACADEMIC JOURNAL PUBLISHING MARKET

This section shall provide the background on the market characteristics from the perspective of both the sellers and the buyers of academic journals. Beginning on the seller's side, we will investigate market shares across publishers and disciplines before turning to the buyer's side, where we provide an overview of journal prices and the conditions at which (university) libraries subscribe to journal content.[14]

The academic journal market may importantly be characterized as a

---

[13]   See more details at https://en.wikipedia.org/wiki/Sci-Hub.

[14]   Henceforth, we will rely on three data sources: First, bibliometric data with journal quality measures from Web of Science in the Journal Citation Report (JCR 2014). Second, data from Bergstrom and McAffee (2013) on journal prices (Table A.2.2 in Appendix 1). Third, metadata from the Directory of Open Access

two-sided market with platform competition, as described by Rochet and Tirole (2003). There are significant network externalities in the sense that authors prefer to publish in academic journals with the largest readership, and readers prefer the journals with the best authors (Bergstrom and Rubinfeld 2010: 138). Since the quality of the journal is commonly proxied by the impact factor (i.e. the frequency of citations, which correlates with readership) and the quality of the authors is equated to the number of publications in journals with a high impact factor, it is very difficult, if not impossible, for an academic library to replace an expensive journal with high impact factor with a cheaper journal in the same research area with a lower impact factor. A publisher who owns a journal with a high impact factor has a strong market position not only with respect to the research- ers (who all seek publication in this journal), but also with respect to the libraries (no library can afford not to subscribe to the journal).

2.2.1   The Supply Side

On the seller's side, publishers organize the selection of scholarly articles as well as the promotion and supply of academic journals in essentially all disciplines. To appreciate the market power that some players enjoy in certain disciplines, we first investigate the market characteristics associ- ated with the (main) players in the market. We then look at individual disciplines or broader research fields to identify their idiosyncratic pub- lishing culture.

2.2.1.1   Characteristics of journal publishers
In the 1950s, commercial publishers began entering the academic journal market. This development was accompanied by a steep increase in the number of scholarly journals.[15] The bibliometric Scopus database cur- rently lists more than 21,500 peer-reviewed journals. The closed catalogue of Thomson Reuter's 'Journal Citation Report' (henceforth 'JCR') lists

---

Journals (DOAJ). See the Appendix for an explanation of the data (Table A.2.1. in Appendix 1 and Table A.2.3 in Appendix 2).

[15]   Bornman and Mutz (2015) find that global scientific output doubles every nine years. Thus, the number of articles published may already be above the socially optimal level. Meho (2007) finds that 90 percent of all journal content is never cited, and 50 percent of all academic works are never read by anybody but the author(s) and reviewers. In this line, Feess and Scheufen (2016) analyze the consequences of an open versus closed access regime, suggesting that OA may correct some of the inefficiencies if we believe that the output level already exceeds the social optimum.

Table 2.1   Distribution of journals and impact factors (IF) by publisher

Publisher	Min IF	Max IF	Mean IF	Number of Journals	Cumulative Market Share
Elsevier	0	45.217	2.745	1,814	0.162
Springer	0	17.737	1.524	1,275	0.277
Wiley-Blackwell	0	115.84	2.276	1,105	0.375
Taylor & Francis	0	20.833	1.111	811	0.448
Sage	0.068	6.837	1.384	493	0.492
All others	0	55.873	1.913	5,672	1.000
Total	0	115.84	1.958	11,170	–

Source: Authors' calculations based on JCR (2014).

11,170 journals with calculated impact factors (JCR 2014).[16] The impact factor (IF) measures the number of citations that a journal receives in a given year for articles published over the last two years in relation to that same number of articles. In other words, the IF is the average number of citations that the articles in a journal received over the last two years. The IF is published annually in the JCR by Thomson Reuter's Web of Science (WoS), together with a number of other impact measures such as the 'five-year impact factor', the h-index or the Eigenfactor.[17] Other databases and proxies for journal reputation in science include 'Scopus' and 'Google Scholar Citations'.[18]

While the number of journals has increased steadily over time, the number of journal publishers has fallen due to numerous mergers and acquisitions. Consequently, today a handful of publishers control the market: Elsevier, Sage, Springer, Taylor & Francis and Wiley-Blackwell. Table 2.1 summarizes the market shares and impact factor characteristics of the big versus the smaller players.

We find that one in two journals listed in the JCR (2014) is owned by one of the big five publishers. In particular, at 1,814 journals or 16.2

---

[16]   The science edition includes 8,003 journals, the social science edition comprises 3,758 journals.

[17]   The h-index (Hirsch 2005) indicates the number of h publications that are cited at least h times. The Eigenfactor rates the total importance of a journal by weighing incoming citations with the rank of the citing journal. See West et al. (2010).

[18]   See Garfield (1955) on the origins of the IF. See Garfield (2003, 2005) or Diamond (2005) for a review.

percent, Elsevier publishes the highest number of journals listed in the JCR (2014). Elsevier is closely followed by Springer (1,275 journals / 11.5 percent) and Wiley-Blackwell (1,105 journals / 9.8 percent) in terms of the number of journals with impact. In terms of journal reputation (impact factor), Elsevier again takes the lead with an average factor of 2.75, compared to an average of 1.91 across the smaller publishers and an average of 1.96 across all journals in the JCR (2014). With an average impact factor of 2.28, journals published by Wiley-Blackwell also enjoy above-average reputation. To summarize: The big five publishers not only host almost half of all academic journals but two of them (Elsevier and Wiley-Blackwell) own a large share of important journals with above-average impact factors.

Given that citation habits and hence citation patterns differ across scientific disciplines,[19] these comparisons are subject to the limitation that some publishers are more active in specific disciplines than in others. Table 2.2 summarizes the mean impact factor and number of journals by publishers and by discipline.[20] Our findings from Table 2.1 reappear in the last row of Table 2.2 as the total number and the mean impact factor across all disciplines. The table also confirms that not all publishers are equally active in each field, which means that one has to be careful when reading publishers' average impact factors as quality signals.[21] While some publishers concentrate on core disciplines – like Sage and Taylor & Francis in 'Health Science' – others divide their activities more evenly across the disciplines (Figure A.2.1(b) in Appendix 1). The distribution across disciplines by publishers (Figure A.2.1(a) in Appendix 1) however shows that Elsevier, Springer and Wiley-Blackwell dominate most fields

---

[19]   Recall that the impact factor mirrors the average number of citations over the last two years for articles of a particular journal in other listed journals. Accordingly, impact factors will be higher in disciplines whose authors cite more articles than those from other disciplines. Consequently, we should be careful when comparing impact factors across disciplines.

[20]   The categorization of disciplines follows the DOAJ, with the abbreviations being: Agri = 'Agriculture and Forestry', Bio = 'Biology and Life Science', Bus = 'Business and Economics', Chem = 'Chemistry', Earth = 'Earth and Environmental Science', Health = 'Health Science', Hist = 'History and Archaeology', LaPo = 'Law and Political Science', Lang = 'Language and Linguistics', Math = 'Mathematics and Statistics', Phys = 'Physics and Astronomy', Social = 'Social Science' and Tech = 'Technology and Engineering'. 'Other' refers to disciplines that do not well fit in any of these fairly broad categories. For more information, see https://doaj.org.

[21]   See Figure A.2.1 in Appendix 1 on the market shares across disciplines by publishers (a) and across publishers by discipline (b).

Table 2.2   Mean impact factor and number of journals by publisher and discipline

Discipline		Elsevier	Springer	Sage	Taylor & Francis	Wiley-Blackwell	All others
Agri	Mean	2.40	1.34	1.19	1.12	1.75	0.81
	N	49	38	2	32	48	245
Bio	Mean	4.04	1.98	2.47	1.72	3.11	3.21
	N	257	164	10	43	151	697
Bus	Mean	1.52	1.07	1.83	0.85	1.20	1.23
	N	96	53	16	40	96	175
Chem	Mean	36.42	1.35	1.66	1.61	3.57	3.18
	N	90	58	1	30	47	220
Earth	Mean	2.46	1.51	2.04	1.19	2.76	1.64
	N	115	104	9	65	78	284
Health	Mean	3.06	2.33	1.86	1.63	3.11	2.61
	N	542	209	96	19	267	1,350
Hist	Mean	0.38	0.72	0.59	0.39	0.42	0.37
	N	5	17	13	22	8	83
LaPo	Mean	0.76	0.61	1.15	0.68	1.22	1.01
	N	6	5	21	33	28	163
Lang	Mean	1.57	0.61	0.91	0.80	0.89	0.57
	N	14	8	11	20	11	106
Math	Mean	1.20	0.89	1.14	0.79	1.30	0.84
	N	67	148	3	36	31	309
Other	Mean	2.16	1.33	1.34	1.17	1.96	1.39
	N	137	119	38	70	81	579
Phys	Mean	2.91	1.47	.	2.51	2.84	2.98
	N	60	70	0	18	12	185
Social	Mean	2.04	1.59	1.23	1.01	1.49	1.31
	N	159	121	247	317	186	688
Tech	Mean	2.32	1.15	1.02	1.18	1.24	1.26
	N	217	161	26	66	61	588
Total	Mean	2.74	1.52	1.38	1.11	2.28	1.91
	N	1,814	1,275	493	811	1,105	5,672

Source: Authors' calculations based on JCR (2014).

when looking at the big five only. In some fields, e.g. in 'Business and Economics' and 'Social Sciences', the big five publishers even command collective market shares in excess of 60 percent. Note, however, that market shares per se do not necessarily equate to market power, as different journals are typically not close substitutes for each other, even within the same discipline. As mentioned before, journals with a high impact factor cannot easily be replaced by other journals from the same research area with a lower impact factor. The reputation of a 'brand' with a high impact factor creates a considerable degree of monopoly power, which allows prices to be raised well above marginal cost. Thus, the market for scholarly journals is characterized by monopolistic competition.[22]

Table 2.2 shows that particularly the impact factors attained by Elsevier are above those reached by 'other' (smaller) publishers and also above the market average. Only in 'Physics and Astronomy' and 'Law and Political Science' do Elsevier journals exhibit a slightly lower impact factor than those of other (smaller) publishers. Comparing impact factors among the top five, we see that Elsevier fails to take the lead only in some disciplines e.g. 'Business and Economics' (highest average impact factor for Sage), 'Health Science' (Wiley-Blackwell), 'History and Archaeology' (Springer), 'Law and Political Science' (Sage) and 'Mathematics and Statistics' (Wiley-Blackwell).

Using boxplots, Figure 2.1 provides a more detailed view of the distribution of the publishers' impact factors in four broad fields of research.[23] The length of the boxes indicates the range of impact factors for the second and third quartile, i.e. for the middle 50 percent, of the observed journals of the respective publisher. The line below (above) the box represents the distribution of the first (fourth) quartile of impact factors. First, we find considerable differences in the impact factors between different fields of research, with the 'Humanities' exhibiting the lowest factors.[24] Second, confirming our findings above, Elsevier dominates all four research fields in terms of the impact factor. The publisher's lead is most pronounced in 'SMT' and somewhat weaker in the other three fields. Wiley-Blackwell tends to come second behind Elsevier. Finally, the smaller publishers' impact factors are far below those of Elsevier and Wiley-Blackwell, though this difference is less evident in 'Life Science'.

These findings suggest considerable differences in the market power of different publishers. The reputation of a journal is not just a signal of

---

[22]   See also Katz (1984) and Edlin and Rubinfeld (2005).

[23]   'SMT' comprises Mathematics, Engineering (Technology), Chemistry, Physics, Computer Science and Geology; 'Humanities' include Language and Linguistics, Philosophy and Religion, as well as History and Archaeology; 'Life Science' covers Medicine, Biology and Agriculture; and 'Social Science' includes Business and Economics, Law and Political Science, Social Science and Education and Psychology. Henceforth, this categorization of publishing cultures or research fields shall serve as a baseline for comparison. We will elaborate further on the characteristics that constitute a publishing culture when discussing the results of our international survey.

[24]   See also Figure 2.4.

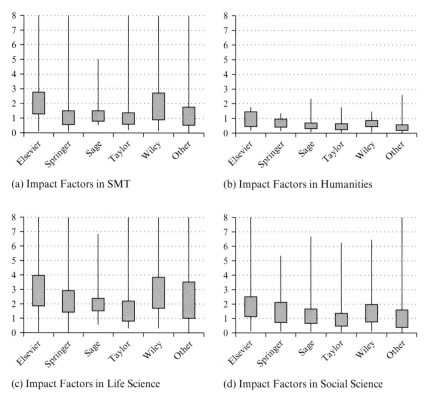

(a) Impact Factors in SMT (b) Impact Factors in Humanities

(c) Impact Factors in Life Science (d) Impact Factors in Social Science

Source: Authors' calculations based on JCR (2014).

Figure 2.1 Boxplot of publishers' impact factors (≤ 8) by research field

quality, it is the multiplier for careers in research. Since in most disciplines and countries, tenure and other types of promotion depend on publications in a closed catalogue of internationally renowned journals, academic authors have no choice but to submit to the best outlets. Given the superior average impact factors of the big five publishers, the reputation and hence the impact factors of their journals are likely to continue increasing in the future: a situation that reinforces itself. We will see that this path dependency is a major obstacle to reform in the academic publishing market.

2.2.1.2 Characteristics of different research fields

As indicated previously, academic fields differ significantly with respect to research and publishing habits. The reasons are threefold: First, the importance of publications in (top tier) journals differs both by discipline

Table 2.3   Impact factor and five-year IF by research field

Research Field		Impact Factor	Five-Year IF	Difference to overall mean[*]	
				IF	FiveIF
SMT	Mean	1.791	2.001	−0.323***	−0.363***
	N	2888	2821		
Humanities	Mean	0.522	0.647	−1.592***	−1.717***
	N	266	248		
Life science	Mean	3.180	3.392	1.065***	1.028***
	N	2652	2556		
Social science	Mean	1.369	1.735	−0.746***	−0.629***
	N	1966	1872		
Total	Mean	2.115	2.364	–	–
	N	7772	7497		

Note: * Difference between the mean IF (Five-Year IF) in each field and the overall mean. *** $p < 0.01$, i.e. for a significance level of at least 1 percent we reject the null hypothesis (no difference between the means).

Source: Authors' calculations based on JCR (2014).

and geographically. Other research outlets may be equally or even more important for reputation. For instance, at least in Germany, publications in books (or commentaries) are of utmost importance for academic careers in law but much less valuable in economics. Second, disciplines also differ considerably in the way that related literature is typically cited and hence also in the number of citations: In a discipline with many citations, impact factors will be higher. We find that a journal in 'Life Science' on average receives almost three times as many citations as a 'Social Science' journal (Table 2.3). In particular, individual research articles in 'Life Science' may be cited up to 100 times, whereas articles in 'Social Science' are very rarely cited more than 30 times. This is why impact factors cannot be compared across disciplines unless these disciplines share a common publishing culture, in which case we may aggregate them into broader research fields. Table 2.3 summarizes the (two-year) impact factor and the five-year impact factor for the four research fields.

Both the two-year and the five-year impact factors differ significantly between disciplines. 'Life Science' has the highest average impact factors among the four fields, with a two-year factor that is 1.065 points higher than the average over all fields. At the bottom end, the average IF of 'Humanities' falls short of the overall average by –1.592 points.

Note that a journal's impact factor is not very indicative of the citation frequency of a typical article contained in it. Even in the top journals, only a few articles are cited very often while most articles are cited very rarely, if ever. For example, data on three different biochemical journals from the mid-1980s show that the most widely cited 15 percent of the articles accounted for half of the citations, and the most widely cited 50 percent of the articles even accounted for 90 percent of the citations (Seglen, 1997: 499). More recent investigations also reveal that a journal's impact factor is not a reliable predictor for the citation frequency of individual articles published in that journal (Haustein and Larivière 2015). While throughout most of the 20th century, the citation rates of individual papers were increasingly linked to the impact factor of their journal, with the spread of electronic journals, this relationship has been weakening. Lozano et al. (2012: 2143f.) have shown that between 1990 and 2009, the share of the 5 percent most cited papers that were published in the top 5 percent journals fell from 2.25 percent to 1.9 percent, whereas the share of the same papers published in the *bottom* 95 percent journals increased from 55 percent to 62 percent. The figures are similar if the line is drawn at 10 percent. To summarize: With digitization and the advent of the internet, the journal impact factor has been losing importance as citations are no longer received only by articles from the top journals.

The third factor to cause differences between academic disciplines is the cited half-life of the papers, i.e. the median age the cited papers had attained by the time the Journal Citation Report was published. The cited half-life provides an indication of the speed at which research in a given field progresses. There are remarkable differences between the disciplines and in particular between more narrowly defined research areas. In particular, we find that the natural sciences have significantly lower average half-lives than non-natural sciences. With an average cited half-life of 4.37 years, Chemistry is the fastest-moving field of research, followed by 'Biology and Life Science' (4.48) and 'Health Science' (4.57). Among the slowest-moving disciplines are 'Language and Linguistics' (8.53 years), 'Law and Political Science' (8.33) and 'Social Science' (7.06).

For these reasons, we will have to take these field-specific characteristics or cultures carefully into account when assessing the role of OA in different research fields. In fact, we will see that specific features of different publishing cultures drive researchers' attitudes towards open access in different fields of research.

2.2.2 The Demand Side: Journal Prices and the Serials Crisis

Academic libraries are the most important buyers of scholarly journals. As already discussed in the Introduction, these libraries have been facing a

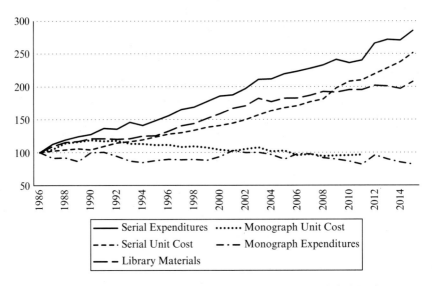

Sources: Serial Unit Cost: Association for Library Collections & Technical Services, 'Prices of U.S. and Foreign Published Materials', various years, with some extrapolation for missing values. All other series: Association of Research Libraries, ARL Statistics Survey, data set 'Expenditure Trends in ARL Libraries 1986-2015'. Note that the series 'monograph expenditures' and 'serials expenditures' were discontinued in 2011 and extended with information on 'one-time expenditures' and 'ongoing expenditures', respectively.

Figure 2.2   Serials and monograph cost development in North-American libraries (inflation-adjusted)

drastic increase in journal prices over the last 30 years, with journal prices increasing faster than the general price level (Figure 2.2). In conjunction with stagnating library budgets, this development has caused the so-called serials crisis: Academic libraries are regularly forced to cancel serials subscriptions and to cut back on new monographs in order to accommodate the rising expenditure on the remaining subscriptions. Discussions on how to cope with the crisis are ripe.

Even though the above graph nicely reflects what triggered the recent discussions on academic publishing, there are some reasons to interpret these figures with caution:

- The data were compiled by libraries associations. If anyone has an incentive to make publications appear expensive, it is them.
- The data are based on surveys. Each year, a different number and set of libraries will have responded, so variations may arise not because

of changes in the underlying statistics but because of changes in response behavior.

- It is unclear how or to what extent the information on serials reflects the fact that the users of libraries are increasingly enjoying access to periodicals both in print and in electronic versions. If libraries lament the increase in periodical expenditures, one must bear in mind that because of the increased electronic availability, users are also receiving more value than before.
- Unit prices for both monographs and serials inevitably refer to averages, i.e. to a basket of publications, which changes each year, based on someone's decision.
- The methodology underlying the data has changed over time. For example, the series 'monograph expenditures' and 'serials expenditures' were discontinued in 2011 but extended with information on 'one-time expenditures' and 'ongoing expenditures', respectively (see 'sources' above).

In some fields – e.g. physics and chemistry – journal subscription prices rose by more than 600 percent between 1984 and 2001 (Edlin and Rubinfeld 2004). Even the director of Harvard Library warned that his library might soon have to cancel journal subscriptions in the face of drastically increasing prices.[25] In 2014, the two most expensive scholarly journals that Harvard Library subscribed to were the monthly *Journal of Comparative Neurology* (USD 28,787 per year) and the weekly *Science* (USD 26,675).[26] In general, given the sharply increasing serial unit cost, libraries have felt compelled to allocate an ever-larger share of their budgets to scholarly journals, causing expenditures on monographs to stagnate. While in 1987, the expenditures of North-American libraries on journals exceeded those for monographs by only 34 percent, in 2011, spending on journals was almost four times that for monographs. The stagnating spending on monographs has been particularly harmful to the humanities, which depend more on books than other disciplines.[27] European academic libraries are experiencing similar problems.[28]

The highest prices are typically charged by commercial, for-profit

---

[25] www.theguardian.com/science/2012/apr/24/harvard-university-journal-publi shers-prices.
[26] http://harvardmagazine.com/2015/01/the-wild-west-of-academic-publishing.
[27] 'On a practical level, how can ever increasing demands for publication as a qualification for tenure and promotion be sustained when scholars find it harder and harder to publish their books?' (Ryan et al., cited in Eve (2014: 112)).
[28] See for example Krujatz (2012: 41) with further references. Regarding the

publishers. Bergstrom reports[29] that in 2013, the mean price per article in for-profit journals was 3.2 times higher than in non-for-profit journals, and that the corresponding ratio for the median price per article was even 4.33:1. Bergstrom and Rubinfeld (2010: 140) compare prices per article and per citation within pairs of economic journals aimed at the same audience, where one is owned by a non-for-profit publisher while the other one is owned by a for-profit publisher. For example, the *American Economic Review*, published by the (non-for-profit) American Economic Association, charges USD 2 per article (USD 1 per citation), whereas *Applied Economics*, published by a for-profit company, charges USD 26 per article (USD 95 per citation). Thus, in this example, the ratios between the non-for-profit and the for-profit publisher are 1:13 for the price per article and 1:95 for the price per citation. The *Journal of Law and Economics*, published by a non-for-profit company, charges USD 4 per article (USD 3 per citation), whereas the *International Review of Law and* Economics, published by a for-profit company, charges USD 29 per article (USD 51 per citation). Similar examples abound. Economists have discussed several interdependent explanations for the increase in journal prices, including the increased concentration of commercial publishers, the bundling of print and electronic journals, and the two-sided nature of the market for academic journals.

Table 2.4 lists the top and bottom five journals in terms of price per article. Several interesting insights can be derived from these figures.

All of the five most expensive journals are published by for-profit publishers, and four of them are published by big five publishers. Three of the five least expensive toll access journals are published by non-for-profit publishers. Even though the most expensive journal (*Advances in Physics*) has an impressive impact factor of 20.88, the table does not provide any more evidence of a clear relationship between a journal's price per article and its impact factor. While the *Journal of Clinical Endocrinology*, one of the five cheapest journals per article, has a high impact factor of 6.209 and two other cheap journals have an impact factor above one, the *International Journal of Manpower*, one of the most expensive ones, has an impact factor of only 0.47.

Table 2.5 reveals that average prices per article in 2013 were significantly above the average in the research area 'SMT' and significantly below the average in 'Life Science'. The price increase over the period 2004–13 was

UK, see for example the publications by the Library and Information Statistics Unit (LISU) at Loughborough University.
[29]   See http://www.journalprices.com.

Table 2.4   Top/bottom five journals by price per article

Journal Title	Publisher	Price per Article	Impact Factor
Advances in Physics	Taylor & Francis	$531.31	20.88
Progress in Crystal Growth and Characterization of Materials	Elsevier	$476.81	3.579
International Journal of Manpower	Emerald	$413.94	0.47
Supramolecular Chemistry	Taylor & Francis	$397.98	2.394
Critical Reviews in Environmental Science and Technology	Taylor & Francis	$379.86	3.468
⋮	⋮	⋮	⋮
Journal of Clinical Endocrinology & Metabolism	Endocrine Society	$0.39	6.209
Commentary	American Jewish Committee	$0.32	0.072
Scientific American	Scientific American Inc	$0.28	1.07
Japanese Journal of Applied Physics	Institute of Pure and Applied Physics	$0.12	1.127
New Scientist	Reed International Business Information Inc.	$0.08	0.284

Source: Authors' calculations based on data from Bergstrom (2013) and JCR (2014).

significantly below average in 'SMT' and significantly above the average in 'Life Science', which suggests a convergence of prices per article over this period.

Finally, Table 2.6 provides some information on the determinants of the prices per article in 2013 and of the price change between 2004 and 2013. Higher prices in 2004 are associated with lower price increases over the next nine years. Thus, there is some evidence of a (small) price convergence among journal articles. Though the age of a journal (measured in years since its first edition) does not have a significant impact on its price per article, older journals experienced a significantly larger price increase over the period 2004–13 than younger ones. Most interestingly, for-profit publishers charged significantly higher prices per article in 2013, but their average price increase over the period 2004–13 was comparatively modest. Articles published by the big five publishers were more expensive in 2013 but experienced less of a price increase over the previous years than those published by smaller companies, associations, university presses, etc. Life science journals are significantly cheaper than journals in other disciplines.

Table 2.5   Price per article (2013) in US $ and price change (2004/2013) in percent by research field

Research Field	Number of Journals	PPA 2013	Difference[*]	Price Change	Difference[*]
SMT	988	24.59	+3.71***	62.92	−9.21*
Humanities	38	24.12	+3.24	61.62	−10.51
Life science	1,829	17.33	−3.56***	81.74	+9.61**
Social science	1,061	21.70	+0.82	66.05	−6.09
Total	3,916	20.88		72.13	

Note: * Difference in the price per article 2013 (in the price change from 2004 to 2013) between each research field and the overall average. * p < 0.1, ** p < 0.05, *** p < 0.01.

Source: Authors' calculations based on data from Bergstrom (2013).

Table 2.6   Determinants of prices per article and price changes

Determinants of Price (Changes)	Price per Article (2013)	Price Change (2004–2015)
Price per article (2004)		−1.008***
		(0.210)
AGE	0.00714	0.0663**
	(0.00453)	(0.0271)
For-profit publisher	15.65***	−18.98***
	(1.009)	(6.958)
BIG5	2.960***	−24.28***
	(1.105)	(6.598)
SMT	0.88	−11.69
	(1.170)	(7.392)
Humanities	2.235	−22.89*
	(1.865)	(12.68)
Life science	−7.016***	3.541
	(0.883)	(5.014)
Observations	4,080	4,080
R-squared	0.118	0.033

Notes: Robust standard errors in parentheses. Social Science is used as reference category. * p < 0.1, ** p < 0.05, *** p < 0.01.

Source: Authors' calculations based on data from Bergstrom (2013) and JCR (2014).

However, subject affiliation does not have a significant impact on the recent price increase.

2.3   THE OPEN ACCESS MOVEMENT

With the advent of the internet and the spread of technologies to digitize information goods, the OA business model appeared on the academic publishing market. The so-called OA movement gained momentum especially thanks to a series of initiatives in 2002 and 2003 which established the principles of OA publishing. In the following, we will first elaborate on the development of OA publishing before addressing some more recent developments and policy aspects of OA publishing.

2.3.1   Open Access Publishing: An Overview

As we have seen, Harnad et al. (2004) distinguish two forms of pure (as opposed to hybrid) OA publishing: the gold road (pure OA journals) and the green road (self-archiving or repository platforms). This distinction provides the structure for this section as we elaborate on the development of each road to OA in turn.

2.3.1.1   The gold road

The gold road of OA publishing has been experiencing phenomenal growth since the year 2000. Pure OA journals are listed in the Directory of Open Access Journals (DOAJ).[30] Excluded from the DOAJ are journals that do not satisfy the definition of pure OA as outlined by the Budapest Open Access Initiative, such as, for example, hybrid OA journals.

As of mid-2016,[31] the DOAJ lists a total of 8,904 OA journals by publishers from 127 countries in 16 different disciplines.[32] Table 2.7 shows the 20 countries with the most OA journals. We find that the top ten (20)

---

[30]   https://doaj.org/search.
[31]   The data was extracted on 30 June 2016. Due to some criticism regarding the seriousness of OA journals the DOAJ in March 2014 tightened its quality criteria and finally removed, in May 2016, from the list around 3,300 journals that no longer qualified as pure OA journals. For more information, see https://doajournals.wordpress.com/2016/05/09/doaj-to-remove-approximately-3300-journals and https://doaj.org/publishers. See also the contributions by Van Noorden (2014) and Baker (2016).
[32]   Note that we follow the categories of disciplines established by the DOAJ throughout this book, distinguishing 15 disciplines and one category referred to as 'other'.

Table 2.7   Number of OA journals by country in 2016 (Top 20)

Rank	Country of Publisher	N	Percent	Cum.
1	Brazil	850	9.55	9.55
2	United Kingdom	725	8.14	17.69
3	United States	673	7.56	25.25
4	Egypt	555	6.23	31.48
5	Spain	516	5.80	37.28
6	Poland	375	4.21	41.49
7	Indonesia	343	3.85	45.34
8	Germany	341	3.83	49.17
9	India	340	3.82	52.99
10	Romania	287	3.22	56.21
11	Italy	286	3.21	59.42
12	Iran	275	3.09	62.51
13	Switzerland	223	2.50	65.02
14	Turkey	216	2.43	67.44
15	Colombia	211	2.37	69.81
16	Russian Federation	150	1.68	71.50
17	France	146	1.64	73.14
18	Canada	137	1.54	74.67
19	Argentina	127	1.43	76.10
20	Netherlands	126	1.42	77.52

Source: Authors' calculations based on DOAJ metadata.

countries contribute more than 50 percent (75 percent) of all OA journals. With a total of 850 (9.55 percent) OA journals, Brazil tops the list, followed closely by publishers from the United Kingdom with 725 (8.14 percent) OA journals and the United States with 673 (7.56 percent). Interestingly, we find the emerging economies Brazil, Egypt, India and Indonesia among the top ten countries in terms of the number of OA journals.

Note that the country of the publisher says little about the language in which the articles are published. On 21 April 2017, the DOAJ listed 9,407 OA journals with 2,471,556 articles. Of these articles, 85.2 percent were in English, 15.5 percent in Portuguese, 12.6 percent in Spanish/Castilian, 5.1 percent in French, 5.1 percent in Spanish, 3.8 percent in Russian, 2.2 percent in Indonesian, 1.8 percent in German and 1.4 percent in Turkish. While there are some concerns about data quality – in some cases, the language indicated as 'full text language' only refers to the abstract – English as the lingua franca clearly dominates, followed at a large distance by Portuguese and different variants of Spanish, whereas other important languages lag behind with only single digit percentage shares.

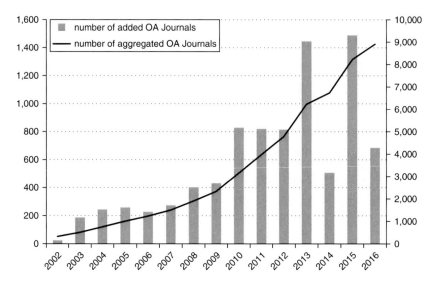

Source: Authors' calculations based on DOAJ metadata.

Figure 2.3   Development of OA journals: 2002–2016

Figure 2.3 shows the development of OA journals over time, both in terms of the number of newly added journals (primary vertical axis) and the aggregate number of journals (secondary vertical axis) from 2002 to 2016.[33] We find that the number of newly added OA journals increased sharply from 2002 to 2013, with 1,442 new journals being added in 2013, but subsequently varied widely over the years 2014 (a plunge to only 505 new journals), 2015 (a peak at 1,487 new journals) and 2016 (another downturn to only 682 new journals).

The dramatic increase in OA journals is due partly to the establishment of new, originary OA journals, and mostly to the conversion of traditional, subscription-based journals to open access.[34] In the first years of the new millennium, most OA articles were published by a small number of specialized publishers. To mention only the most important ones: BioMed Central, based in London, was already founded in 2000 with a focus on Biology, Clinical Medicine and Health. In 2008, it was acquired by one of the big academic publishers, Springer Nature. As of 2017,

---

[33]   Note that 330 OA journals existed already before the year 2002, marking the starting point for the existing number of OA journals.
[34]   For more details see the informative study by Solomon et al. (2016).

BioMed Central holds 300 journals comprising 121,387 articles.[35] In 2003, the non-for-profit organization Public Library of Science (PLOS) based in San Francisco launched the OA journal *PLOS Biology*, which has achieved one of the highest impact factors in this field. Today, PLOS owns only eight journals with articles from across science and medicine. However, at 187,521 articles, the mega-journal *PLOS ONE* makes its distributor the largest OA publisher in the world. The Multidisciplinary Publishing Institute (MDPI) located in Basel, Switzerland, was established already in 1996 and focuses on Science and Medicine but also includes articles from Social Sciences, Arts and Humanities, Business and Economics and Computer Science and Mathematics. Today, the MDPI's portfolio comprises 149 OA journals with 92,028 articles. Copernicus Publications from Göttingen, Germany, with a focus on Earth Science, launched their first OA journal in 2001. Their portfolio comprises 38 OA journals, 18 of which are subject to an interactive public peer review, and 59,412 articles. Interestingly, two large OA publishers reside outside of Europe or the US. The Hindawi Publishing Corporation is based in Cairo, Egypt, was founded in 1997 and has been granting open access to all of its journals since 2007. Hindawi currently owns 563 OA journals covering a broad range of disciplines, with 180,572 articles. Finally, Medknow Publications was founded in 1997 in Mumbai, India, with the mission 'to help medical societies disseminate research, thus supporting the transformation of research into knowledge'.[36] Having been acquired by Wolters Kluwer in December 2011, Medknow today publishes 66 OA journals with 71,979 articles available.

More recently, traditional commercial academic publishers have become interested in open access. In some cases, they have established hybrid journals, where open access is granted to individual articles, provided the author has paid a corresponding APC. As of September 2017, the DOAJ reports the following number of pure OA journals published by big commercial academic publishers: Elsevier – 362, De Gruyter Open – 324, Springer – 198, Wolters Kluwer Medknow Publications – 117, SAGE Publishing – 106, Taylor & Francis Group – 62, and Wiley – 561. In terms of articles, only Elsevier (103,769 articles) and Wolters Kluwer Medknow Publications (77,868) are among the top ten of OA publishers.

Looking at the number and distribution of OA journals, we find significant differences between the disciplines. With a total of 2,109 journals,

---

[35] These and the following figures use data collected from the DOAJ on 13 April 2017.
[36] http://www.medknow.com/aboutus.asp.

the field of 'Health Science' accounts for 24 percent of all OA journals, followed by 'Social Science' with 1,204 (14 percent) and 'Technology and Engineering' with 832 (9 percent). Table 2.8 furthermore reveals differences among the disciplines with regard to the degrees of internationalization, of the use of peer-review, of the stipulation of rules on plagiarism and of the imposition of publishing and/or submission fees on authors. First, internationalization refers to whether a journal is published at least in English (several journals appear in more than one language). By this measure, the share of international journals ranges from 51 percent in 'History and Archaeology' to 79 percent in 'Health Science' and 81 percent in 'Technology and Engineering'. Second, almost half of all OA journals have some kind of peer-review system,[37] with shares ranging from 31 percent in 'Mathematics and Statistics' to 56 percent in 'Technology and Engineering'. Given the importance of a thorough peer-review system to the quality of academic works, these numbers appear somewhat low. Third, only 27 percent of OA journals have a policy on plagiarism.[38] Fourth, moving from a closed access system with subscription prices for readers to an open access model necessarily requires that somebody other than the readers pay for the journal's services. As outlined earlier, OA originally refers to an 'author pays' model, where authors are charged up to USD 3,000 per article upon submission or publication. Table 2.8 shows that only 16 percent of all OA journals actually charge authors either article processing fees (APCs) or a submission fee, ranging from four percent in 'Agriculture' to 35 percent in 'Philosophy'. The low figures suggest that OA journal publishers must have other sources of income. These include grants (PLOS), print subscriptions (Hindawi) and advertising (Medknow) (Scheufen 2015: 78–79). Nevertheless, most OA journals with a higher impact factor use some form of publication fee, which in the case of PLOS journals, for example, range from USD 1,495 (*PLOS ONE*) to USD 2,900 (*PLOS Biology* and *PLOS Medicine*).

Finally, the table also shows the average cited half-life per discipline. We find that by this measure, research progresses faster in natural science (cited half-life is less than five years) than in non-natural science, especially in fields like 'Business and Economics' (6.94), 'Social Sciences' (7.06), 'Law and Political Science' (8.33), and 'Languages' (8.53).

This leads us again to the crucial question: In the different disciplines

---

[37] Peer-review may refer to either a single, double or double-blind peer-review system.

[38] Note that a lack of quality thresholds and the threat of plagiarism are two of the most important points of criticism levelled at the OA movement. We will elaborate further especially on the first aspect in our survey analysis.

Table 2.8   Number and characteristics of OA journals by discipline (2016)

Discipline	All Journals		International		Peer-Review		Plagiarism		Author Fees		Cited Half-life	
	N	Share	N	Share	N	Share	N	Share	N	Share	N	Mean
Agri	373	0.04	287	0.77	166	0.45	88	0.24	14	0.04	35	6.47
Art	198	0.02	133	0.67	101	0.51	34	0.17	31	0.16	.	.
Bio	495	0.06	407	0.82	226	0.46	164	0.33	109	0.22	115	4.48
Bus	412	0.05	292	0.71	186	0.45	100	0.24	61	0.15	5	6.94
Chem	143	0.02	124	0.87	63	0.44	56	0.39	38	0.27	27	4.37
Earth	487	0.05	335	0.69	218	0.45	117	0.24	48	0.10	35	6.42
Health	2,109	0.24	1,670	0.79	1,074	0.51	847	0.40	247	0.12	99	4.57
Hist	265	0.03	136	0.51	114	0.43	28	0.11	49	0.18	.	.
LaPo	371	0.04	230	0.62	197	0.53	76	0.20	51	0.14	4	8.33
Lang	539	0.06	319	0.59	212	0.39	65	0.12	25	0.05	3	8.53
Math	394	0.04	316	0.80	121	0.31	88	0.22	106	0.27	20	5.99
Other	534	0.06	353	0.66	206	0.39	99	0.19	161	0.30	344	5.19
Phil	391	0.04	245	0.63	174	0.45	76	0.19	138	0.35	.	.
Phys	157	0.02	136	0.87	87	0.55	71	0.45	40	0.25	26	4.63
Social	1,204	0.14	734	0.61	508	0.42	190	0.16	108	0.09	74	7.06
Tech	832	0.09	678	0.81	468	0.56	329	0.40	239	0.29	50	4.66
Total	8,904	1.00	6,395	0.72	4,121	0.46	2,428	0.27	1,465	0.16	837	5.27

Source: Authors' calculations based on DOAJ metadata and JCR (2014).

what are academic scholars' motives to submit articles to OA journals? Of course, scholars want to be read and cited, and OA may promote wider readership. However, as mentioned before, a journal's impact factor is among the most relevant indicators of its reputation. As scientific careers in most disciplines are driven by the reputation a researcher has accumulated from her publication record,[39] the impact factor is also an important indicator of a journal's market power. In other words, a well-reputed journal may expect to receive more and better articles as the inherent reward structure urges scientist to choose this outlet. Hence, reputation and impact factors are mutually self-reinforcing.

Comparing OA versus CA journals in terms of impact factors yields interesting insights regarding their relevance in various disciplines.[40] Table 2.9 summarizes the total number and the mean (two-year and five-year) impact factors of OA versus CA journals as listed in the JCR (2014). We find that of the 11,111 journals with impact, only around 8 percent (900) are open access. However, this share varies widely across disciplines.

A more detailed view on distributional measures of the IF differences between the two types of outlets supports the perception of an 'impact factor advantage' of established CA over OA journals. Figure 2.4 shows a boxplot of the impact factor by discipline, comparing OA and CA journals. Along the horizontal axis, we have the absolute number and the mean IF of all WoS listed journals for both OA and CA journals, as also contained in Table 2.9. The boxplot itself depicts the upper and lower bounds in terms of the IF, as well as the first and third quartile. For ease of presentation, the IF is capped at the upper end at ten.

Similar to our findings from Section 2.2 (Table 2.4), we find evidence of differences in publishing cultures between the research fields.[41] In particular, 'Life Science' but also 'SMT' disciplines dominate the other fields in terms of the impact factor. Nevertheless, within the research fields, the picture confirms a significant impact factor advantage for CA versus OA journals. While the IF distributions are still somewhat similar across the

---

[39] In particular, a scientist's reputation capital can be measured as the sum of all articles weighted by the impact factor of the journals they are published in. See Section 2.1.1 for details on the reward structure in science.

[40] Given that the publishing cultures differ considerably, especially with respect to citation patterns and hence also impact factors, differences between disciplines must be interpreted carefully. Nevertheless, a comparison of both regimes within the same field can reveal why we observe more OA in some fields than in others.

[41] See Figure A.2.2 in Appendix 2 for a boxplot of OA versus CA journals by research field. Similarly, Table A.2.4 in Appendix 2 reveals significant differences in the impact factor between OA and CA by research field.

Table 2.9   Impact factors of open versus closed access journals

Discipline		All WoS Journals		Open Access		Closed Access		Difference[*]	
		IF	FiveIF	IF	FiveIF	IF	FiveIF	IF	FiveIF
Agri	Mean	1.182	1.407	0.745	0.851	1.256	1.491	0.511***	0.640***
	N	413	395	60	52	353	343		
Bio	Mean	3.158	3.417	2.627	2.897	3.228	3.480	0.601**	0.582**
	N	1,309	1,276	152	138	1,157	1,138		
Bus	Mean	1.240	1.742	0.671	0.878	1.253	1.762	0.582***	0.884***
	N	473	453	10	10	463	443		
Chem	Mean	2.974	3.150	1.455	1.522	3.072	3.249	1.618***	1.727***
	N	445	437	27	25	418	412		
Earth	Mean	1.863	2.201	1.633	1.952	1.889	2.226	0.256**	0.274**
	N	652	629	66	59	586	570		
Health	Mean	2.700	2.849	2.146	2.393	2.764	2.896	0.619***	0.503***
	N	2,464	2,341	254	216	2,210	2,125		
Hist	Mean	0.439	0.501	0.216	0.189	0.444	0.506	0.227	0.318
	N	147	129	3	2	144	127		
LaPo	Mean	0.990	1.175	0.655	0.747	1.002	1.192	0.347	0.445
	N	256	243	9	9	247	234		
Lang	Mean	0.722	0.944	0.594	0.949	0.725	0.944	0.132	−0.006
	N	170	161	5	5	165	156		
Math	Mean	0.914	1.087	1.010	1.362	0.910	1.078	−0.100	−0.284
	N	594	571	22	19	572	552		

Other	Mean	1.516	1.692	1.461	1.681	1.522	1.693	0.061***	0.011***
	N	1,020	974	105	101	915	873		
Phys	Mean	2.631	2.694	3.316	3.550	2.568	2.621	−0.748	−0.929
	N	345	343	29	27	316	316		
Social	Mean	1.350	1.723	1.045	1.193	1.367	1.751	0.322***	0.559***
	N	1,709	1,625	94	83	1,615	1,542		
Tech	Mean	1.442	1.663	1.086	1.138	1.464	1.693	0.379	0.555**
	N	1,114	1,093	64	60	1,050	1,033		
Total	Mean	1.958	2.198	1.769	1.977	1.974	2.216	0.205***	0.238***
	N	11,111	10,670	900	806	10,211	9,864		

Notes: 'Art' and 'Phil' not reported due to the low number of journals listed in these fields by the JCR (2014).
* Difference in the IF (FiveIF) between CA versus OA journals. * $p < 0.1$, ** $p < 0.05$, *** $p < 0.01$.

Source: Authors' calculations based on DOAJ metadata and JCR (2014).

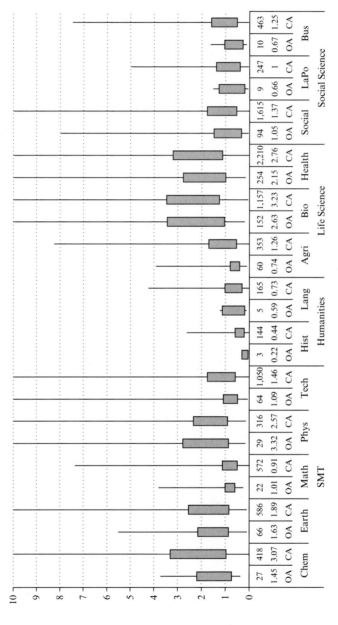

Note: The first (second) line below the horizontal axis shows the absolute number (mean IF) of all WoS listed journals for both OA and CA journals. 'Art' and 'Phil' are omitted due to the low number of journals listed in these fields by the JCR (2014).

Source: Authors' calculations based on DOAJ metadata and JCR (2014).

Figure 2.4 Boxplot of the impact factor (≤ 10) by discipline or field: OA vs. CA journals

two regimes e.g. in 'Biology and Life Science' or in 'Health Science', much larger discrepancies exist for example in 'Business and Economics' and 'Technology and Engineering'. In the latter fields, the third quartile of the impact factor for OA journals is just about level with the first quartile for CA journals. That is, while 75 percent of all OA journals in 'Business and Economics' ('Technology and Engineering') have an IF of no more than1.04 (1.08), this applies to only around 40 percent of CA journals (see Table A.2.1 in Appendix 1).

All of the above once more illustrates the considerable differences both in the number and the impact of OA versus CA journals across different disciplines. Let us now turn to the green road as the alternative way of providing free and unrestricted access to academic works.

2.3.1.2 The green road

The green road refers to the self-archiving of research papers by the authors before, after or independently of publication in a traditional scholarly journal. The simplest way of self-archiving is for an author to deposit a research article on her personal homepage. However, articles posted to the web in such a manner are difficult to find via search engines. For that reason, the green road has evolved in particular through the establishment of *disciplinary (subject) repositories*, which aggregate research papers in specific disciplines, and *institutional repositories*, which aggregate research papers authored by the members of certain institutions, such as universities, faculties, departments and research institutes. Many of these repositories comply with the Open Archives Initiative Protocol for Metadata Harvesting (OAI-PMH) of 1999, which ensures the interoperability of different repositories for the purpose of locating their contents (Suber 2012: 56; Awre 2006).[42] More recently, we have seen the emergence of *academic social networks* such as Research Gate, Mendeley and Academia, which are typically funded by venture capital and often invite the uploading even of published articles (Björk 2016).

For copyright reasons, the content of disciplinary and institutional repositories is subject to different degrees of open access. Sometimes the abstracts are freely available but the full texts are not. Even when the full

---

[42] There is still room for improvement though. In the US, the SHARE initiative, founded in 2013 by the Association of Research Libraries, the Association of American Universities and the Association of Public and Land-grant Universities, has been working on this problem (www.share-research.org). The Confederation of Open Access Repositories (COAR) started in 2009 as an EU-sponsored project and has become a global institution with a focus on repository interoperability (www.coar-repositories.org).

text is accessible, sometimes this is on a 'read only' basis, whereas in other cases, the access rights extend to downloading, copying, distributing and printing the text. Some articles are available only temporarily, others permit permanent access. Some articles become available immediately after publication in a CA journal, others only after some 'embargo period'. Future challenges of the green road include data curation and long-term preservation (Archambault et al. 2014: iii).

Publishers of traditional journals are naturally concerned that self-archiving may harm their business model. Many journals in health science, but also in other life sciences, discourage self-archiving *prior to publication* in a journal by applying the 'Ingelfinger rule', which bans the publication of articles that have previously been published elsewhere (Krujatz 2012: 28–29). Self-archiving of articles *post publication* is also restricted in several ways by the journal publishers as the copyright-holders. The Sherpa/Romeo database, which covers journals by 2,214 publishers from around world, distinguishes four policies toward self-archiving, which are assigned different colours:[43]

1) Green: 39 percent of the publishers allow both *pre-print and post-print self-archiving*. In many cases authors may archive the final draft after the referee process but not the final publisher's version (the PDF file of the printed pages). Other restrictions with respect to the timing of post-print archiving may apply. Publishers often impose an embargo period of six, 12 or more months between publication and archiving. Some publishers accept self-archiving immediately after publication on the author's personal website but not in an open access repository.

2) Blue: 33 percent of the publishers allow *only post-print self-archiving*, i.e. archiving of the final draft post-refereeing. While some publishers permit their authors to archive the final publisher's PDF after an embargo period, others accept only authors' final versions for self-archiving, but immediately after publication.

3) Yellow: 7 percent of the publishers *only allow pre-print self-archiving*, i.e. pre-refereeing.

4) White: 21 percent of the publishers *do not formally permit self-archiving*.

Though the Sherpa/Romeo database is very useful for understanding the different publishers' policies on self-archiving, the actual detailed rules

---

[43]   www.sherpa.ac.uk/romeo/statistics.php?la=en&fIDnum=|&mode=simple; accessed on 20 June 2016.

vary considerably within these four categories, so careful interpretation is required.

The history of the green road of open access already began in 1991, when physicist Paul Ginsparg at the Los Alamos National Laboratory established arXiv, an open access repository which is currently owned by Cornell University Library and provides open access to over one million e-prints in physics, mathematics, computer science, quantitative biology, quantitative finance and statistics. In 1994, Wayne Marr and Michael Jensen launched another influential open access repository, the 'Social Science Research Network' (SSRN), which includes an Electronic Paper Collection of currently over half a million downloadable full text documents. In 1997, Stevan Harnard, one of the early promoters of open access in the US, launched the repository 'cogprints', which specializes in psychology, neuroscience, linguistics and computer science. Next, RePEc is a decentralized database of working papers, pre-prints, journal articles and software components in the field of economics. Launched in 1997, it is sponsored by the Research Division of the Federal Reserve Bank of St. Louis and provides links to over 1,200,000 full text articles, most of which are freely downloadable. In the same year, the NEC Research Institute at Princeton established CiteSeer, a scientific literature digital library and search engine with a focus on computer and information science. Other large subject-based repositories include the Bepress Legal Repository, established in 2004 by Robert Cooter and Aaron Edlin in Berkeley, and PhilPapers, the primary open access archive in philosophy, which is being developed since 2006 by David Bourget and David Chalmers of the Australian National University. Since 2013, PhilPapers has been administered by the Centre for Digital Philosophy at the University of Western Ontario. Last but not least, launched in 2000, PubMed Central (PMC) is the US National Institute of Health's digital archive of biomedical and life science articles. It provides free full text reading access; however, only some of the articles are distributed under a Creative Commons or similar license, the rest are restricted with respect to usage and download rights. For that reason, articles in PMC are not considered green OA in the narrow sense as defined by the European Commission (Archambault et al. 2014: 24). As of 2016, the archive contains about 3.9 million articles.

Many smaller subject repositories exist besides these major venues. However, Björk (2013: 14) reports that arXiv and PMC together account for 94 percent of all self-archived manuscripts in subject repositories. The author explains the success of subject repositories in a limited number of areas by two factors: (1) a strong working paper or pre-print culture that existed already prior to the internet (arXiv, SSRN, RePEc), and (2) a

Table 2.10   Types of repositories and their distribution among the top 10 countries

Rank	Country	Disciplinary Repositories	Institutional Repositories	Other Repositories	Total
1	USA	80	377	39	496
2	UK	44	201	7	252
3	Japan	–	205	6	211
4	Germany	13	178	4	195
5	Spain	18	87	20	125
6	France	18	88	13	119
7	Italy	7	102	1	110
8	Brazil	10	74	8	92
9	Poland	8	77	7	92
10	Canada	10	69	1	80
	World	297	2,856	187	3,340

Source: OpenDOAR, accessed on 20 April 2017.

corresponding mandate by the dominant research funder, i.e. the obligation to publish a funded paper OA (PMC) (Björk 2013: 16).

One recent strategy of traditional commercial journal publishers to avoid negative externalities from green OA is to acquire successful OA repositories. For example, Elsevier acquired Mendeley in 2013 and SSRN in 2016.

In addition to the disciplinary repositories and academic social networks, a considerable number of *institutional repositories* have also emerged. They typically host not only journal articles but also theses and dissertations, books and book chapters, unpublished reports and working papers, multimedia content, and so on. The global number of all types of repositories increased from 902 in May 2007 to 3,340 in April 2017.[44] Table 2.10 reveals that most repositories are institutional ones, and it shows the allocation of repositories among the top ten countries. The USA host 496 repositories, i.e. about 15 percent of all repositories globally, followed by the UK (252), Japan (211) and Germany (195).

Most repositories include journal articles (Table 2.11a). Among the top

---

[44]   We refer to the statistics by OpenDOAR, a registry administered by the University of Nottingham, UK, which applies strict criteria regarding the acceptance of suggested entries (see www.opendoar.org/suggestionschart.html). The alternative register, ROAR, administered by the University of Southampton, UK, is based on automatic harvesting and contains some duplicates. Since not all repositories are registered, some repositories are missing from both registries.

Table 2.11a   *Most frequent content types* in repositories in the top 10 countries and in the world*

Rank	Country	Journal Articles	Theses and Dissertations	Books, Chapters and Sections	Unpublished Reports and Working Papers	Conference and Workshop Papers	Multimedia and Audio-visual Material	Total
1	USA	292	229	137	202	150	231	496
2	UK	177	79	86	86	97	62	252
3	Japan	192	101	38	90	39	20	211
4	Germany	132	139	109	101	90	41	195
5	Spain	85	66	67	32	34	27	125
6	France	82	80	57	60	62	15	119
7	Italy	81	51	65	26	69	8	110
8	Brazil	57	54	35	17	20	19	92
9	Poland	74	29	75	16	18	20	92
10	Canada	54	44	25	37	34	22	80
	World	2,370	1,854	1,268	1,170	1,119	745	3,340

Notes: * Most repositories hold several content types. Other content types, such as other special items, learning objects, bibliographic references, datasets, patents and software are not included.

Source: OpenDOAR, accessed on 20 April 2017.

ten countries, only Germany features more repositories that host theses and dissertations than ones that host journal articles, and in Poland more repositories host books, chapters and sections than journal articles.

Table 2.11b provides an overview of the global numbers of repositories with specific content types in each discipline. Note that these numbers do not indicate the importance of the green road in different disciplines since the mere count of repositories ignores their vastly different sizes (see above). Only in 'History' do repositories that host journal articles fail to constitute the largest group.

Around 70 percent of all repositories rely on English as their main or only language, followed at some distance by Spanish (12.5 percent), German (7.5 percent), French (6.7 percent), Japanese (6.3 percent), Portuguese (4.9 percent) and Chinese (3.4 percent) (Table 2.12a). Of course, it could be argued that the predominance of English may be due to the very large number of repositories located in the US and the UK. However, even without these countries, around 48.8 percent of the repositories in the remaining countries rely on English as their main or only language, which stresses the importance of English as the lingua franca in academia.

Table 2.12b indicates the importance of English and other languages in the repositories of different disciplines.

English as the main or only language dominates most strongly in Science (Biology: 100 percent; Earth Science: 87.5 percent; Physics: 83.2 percent; Chemistry: 80.6 percent), whereas it is least dominant in the Humanities (Philosophy and Religion: 63.8 percent; History: 66.2 percent; Language and Literature: 67.8 percent). Surprisingly, at 81.6 percent, repositories devoted to the Arts rely strongly on English. However, if we again disregard repositories from the US and the UK, English loses its importance in this discipline. With respect to the other disciplines, the ranking remains more or less the same. Outside of the US and the UK, English is most prevalent as the main or only language in Science (Biology: 100 percent; Earth Science: 82 percent; Physics: 78.8 percent; Chemistry: 75.6 percent) and is again used the least in the Humanities (History: 46.8 percent; Philosophy and Religion: 52.6 percent; Language and Literature: 58.4 percent).

2.3.2   Recent Developments

2.3.2.1   General development
We have already mentioned that since the late 1980s, a number of fundamental changes to the scientific publishing business have brought new challenges for publishers, libraries, academic authors and their

Table 2.11b   Content types of repositories in different disciplines

Discipline	Journal Articles	Theses and Dissertations	Books, Chapters and Sections	Unpublished Reports and Working Papers	Conference and Work-shop Papers	Multimedia and Audio-visual Materials	Total
Agri	109	77	53	65	64	33	147
Art	58	39	45	24	30	55	103
Bio	117	83	53	49	62	35	155
Bus	180	158	95	109	97	40	249
Chem	73	61	40	28	43	18	98
Earth	70	34	38	48	40	25	88
Health	250	161	97	115	104	53	326
Hist	117	71	130	58	44	122	246
LaPo	154	114	90	100	75	49	226
Lang	92	71	76	38	47	45	146
Math	100	75	48	41	57	24	122
Phil	83	66	68	36	39	31	127
Phys	86	71	46	40	53	25	107
Social	139	104	88	88	62	45	192
Tech	182	152	85	95	112	42	235

Source: OpenDOAR, accessed on 20 April 2017.

Table 2.12a   Main languages in repositories in the top 10 countries and in the world

Rank	Country	English	Spanish	German	French	Japanese	Portuguese	Chinese	Total
1	USA	495	13	6	7	2	3	4	496
2	UK	252	5	3	6	–	–	–	252
3	Japan	118	–	4	1	207	–	4	211
4	Germany	116	1	182	1	1	–	–	195
5	Spain	46	120	1	5	–	4	–	125
6	France	66	2	1	109	–	–	2	119
7	Italy	86	2	–	3	–	–	–	110
8	Brazil	26	13	–	–	–	91	–	92
9	Poland	29	–	4	1	–	–	–	92
10	Canada	70	–	3	29	–	–	1	80
	World	2,337	418	252	223	212	165	114	3,340

Source: OpenDOAR, accessed on 20 April 2017.

Table 2.12b   Main languages in repositories in different disciplines

Discipline	English	Spanish	German	French	Japanese	Portuguese	Chinese	Total
Agri	108	25	2	12	5	5	8	147
Art	84	10	9	6	2	2	2	103
Bio	123	16	9	13	1	4	8	123
Bus	176	28	27	25	8	6	7	249
Chem	79	5	6	11	–	3	8	98
Earth	77	11	6	8	3	2	2	88
Health	239	43	13	19	34	17	9	326
Hist	163	28	19	19	7	4	7	246
LaPo	165	22	20	20	8	10	6	226
Lang	99	15	18	15	6	4	11	146
Math	94	9	9	15	1	5	2	122
Phil	81	10	15	4	3	2	6	127
Phys	89	3	6	11	–	5	9	107
Social	145	31	23	25	6	6	5	192
Tech	178	30	21	22	15	8	17	235

Source: OpenDOAR, accessed on 20 April 2017.

readers: the serials crisis, the development of digitization and the advent of the internet. Rooted in the 1980s and 1990s, three highly influential initiatives by academic scholars, representatives of research libraries and research sponsors from all over the world to foster open access in academic publishing came to light at the beginning of the new millennium: the 'Budapest Open Access Initiative' (February 2002), the 'Bethesda Statement on Open Access Publishing' (June 2003), and the 'Berlin Declaration on Open Access to Knowledge in the Sciences and Humanities' (October 2003). Since then, research sponsors, academic libraries and political authorities in many countries as well as at the European and international level have engaged in strategies to foster open access in academic publishing.[45]

These initiatives were met not only with appreciation (mostly from the academic community) but also with disapproval. In particular, the commercial academic publishers faced a threat to their business model. In Germany, Roland Reuß, a professor of German Studies at the University of Heidelberg, in 2009 initiated the 'Heidelberg Appeal', which not only criticized the GoogleBooks program and YouTube for copyright infringement but also rejected the support for OA by the 'Alliance of German Scientific

[45]   See, for example, https://open-access.net/DE-EN/information-on-open-access/positions-on-open-access.

Organisations', arguing that it conflicts with the freedom of literature, art and science as a major constitutional asset.[46] After a few weeks, this appeal had received more than 2,600 signatures from authors and publishers but had also provoked a lot of criticism from other scholarly authors.[47]

In January 2012, Timothy Gowers, a British mathematician at the University of Cambridge and recipient of the Fields Medal, initiated a boycott against Elsevier, the leading publisher of academic journals. The participants refused to edit, review or submit articles to Elsevier publications. The boycott was motivated, amongst other factors, by exorbitant journal subscription prices, the practice of bundling journals ('big deals'), and Elsevier's active lobbying against open access. As of 14 August 2016, no fewer than 16,157 scholars have joined the boycott. In the same year, Timothy Gowers launched the new open access journal *Discrete Analysis* as an arXiv overlay journal. This means that authors will submit links to arXiv pre-prints, the submissions will be refereed, and the editors decide which papers will be published virtually free of charge for readers and authors. At most, authors contribute USD 10 per submission to cover the cost of the software used for managing the referee process. By editing this journal, Gowers intends to demonstrate that 'if you trust authors to do their own typesetting and copy-editing to a satisfactory standard, with the help of suggestions from referees, then the cost of running a mathematics journal can be at least two orders of magnitude lower than the cost incurred by traditional publishers'.[48]

2.3.2.2   Policy development
The global growth of OA publishing in academia essentially owes to three groups of players who modified the rules of the game for academic authors: national parliaments and governments via new legislation or through less formal means of influence, the major research funders, and the research institutions. In the following, we will discuss the policies pursued by each type of players.[49]

2.3.2.2.1 Support by national parliaments and governments and by the European Commission   Regarding new *legislation*, the *US* was the

---

[46]   The English text is available at www.textkritik.de/urheberrecht/index_engl. htm.
[47]   See, for example, www.perlentaucher.de/essay/open-excess-der-heidelberger-appell.html (unfortunately only available in German).
[48]   For more details, see https://gowers.wordpress.com/2015/09/10/discrete-ana lysis-an-arxiv-overlay-journal.
[49]   See, for example, the excellent overview in Archambault et al. (2014: 5–16).

first country to adopt a national OA mandate, i.e. to oblige authors by law to grant open access to specified articles. The Consolidated Appropriations Act, 2008 (HR 2764), requires all researchers funded by the National Institutes of Health (NIH) to submit – no later than 12 months after the official date of publication – an electronic version of their final, peer-reviewed manuscripts to the National Library of Medicine's PubMed Central. The Federal Research Public Access Act (FRPAA), proposed in 2006, 2010 and 2012, intended to extend the national OA mandate beyond medicine to all agencies with extramural research expenditures of at least USD 100 million. However, the proposal never made it into law and was succeeded by the discussion on the Fair Access to Science and Technology Act (FASTR), a reinforced version of the FRPAA, which was introduced in Congress in February 2013, unanimously approved by the Committee on Homeland Security and Governmental Affairs in July 2015 and remains pending as of 2017. These initiatives are supplemented by corresponding legislation at the state level.

In *Spain*, Article 37 ('Open Access Dissemination') of the National Law on Science, Technology and Innovation 14/2011 stipulates that Spanish institutions should develop interoperable OA repositories, and mandates Spanish researchers who are mainly funded by the national government to deposit the final version of papers accepted for publication in such a repository within 12 months. There is also some corresponding legislation at the level of the autonomous regional governments.

Germany in October 2013 amended Article 38(4) of its Copyright Act. The amendment came into force in January 2014 and has introduced an inalienable right, following an embargo period of 12 months, to secondary publication for research that is publicly funded by at least 50 percent. The exact wording of Article 38(4) is:

> (4) The author of a scientific contribution which is the result of a research activity publicly funded by at least fifty per cent and which has appeared in a collection which is published periodically at least twice per year has the right, even if he has granted the publisher or editor an exclusive right of use, to make the contribution available to the public in the accepted manuscript version upon expiry of 12 months after first publication, unless this serves a commercial purpose. The source of the first publication shall be indicated. Any deviating agreement to the detriment of the author shall be ineffective.

Italy in October 2013 approved the Law 112/2013, which introduced an open access mandate for research publicly funded by at least 50 percent. The authors retain the choice between the gold road and the green road. In the latter case, the embargo period is 18 months for scientific, technical and medical disciplines, and 24 months for the humanities and social sciences (Moscon 2014).

The *Netherlands* in July 2015 amended their Copyright Act in order to provide a legal basis for academic authors to make their research results available globally in open access. The new Article 25fa Copyright Act states:

> The maker of a short scientific work, the research for which has been paid for in whole or in part by Dutch public funds, shall be entitled to make that work available to the public for no consideration following a reasonable period of time after the work was first published, provided that clear reference is made to the source of the first publication of the work.[50]

Some *Latin American countries*, including Argentina and Peru in 2013 and Mexico in 2014, have enacted national laws to require the results of state-funded research to be deposited in OA digital repositories.[51] Additionally, a number of other countries feature national legislative activities on OA mandates that are less detailed (Lithuania) or are as of 2016 still at the proposal stage (Brazil, Poland, Denmark).

Some countries, of which we only discuss a few informative examples, furthermore pursue national policies *below the level of legislation*. The most remarkable example is the *United Kingdom*, which began discussions on promoting open access publishing in academia very early on (Tickel 2016). Parliament already recommended a shift to OA publishing in 2004 but the initiative was discouraged by the government at the time. It was not until 2012, following strong advocacy for gold OA in the Finch Report, that the government implemented the following strategy: (1) the provision of additional funds for research-intensive institutions to purchase access to OA journals (so-called 'block grants' to cover APCs) and to build institutional repositories; (2) varying embargo periods for green OA depending on the discipline; (3) green OA is only acceptable if no funds are available for gold OA. Based on these principles, the Research Councils revised their policies in April 2013, and the Higher Education Funding Council for England stated in March 2014 that only institutions which grant OA to almost all of their publications will be eligible for the next Research Excellence Framework.

According to the 'National Principles for Open Access Policy Statement' formulated in October 2012 by *Ireland*'s National Steering Committee on

---

[50]   See http://openaccess.nl/en/events/amendment-to-copyright-act.
[51]   See www.unesco.org/new/en/communication-and-information/portals-and-platforms/goap/access-by-region/ latin-america-and-the-caribbean.

Open Access, research output fully or partially funded by the Irish government must be deposited in OA repositories. This green OA mandate is supplemented by an encouragement of gold OA. Green OA benefits from a well-established network of interoperable institutional repositories of the seven university libraries and other research repositories in Ireland. For some years, the research content has been accessible via one national portal (RIAN).

The *Swedish* National Library has been running the national OA program 'OpenAccess.se' since 2006. The program promotes open access to works produced by Swedish researchers, teachers and students by supporting green and gold OA, by providing information and advice, as well as by developing suitable infrastructure, services and policy coordination. Commissioned by the government, the Swedish Research Council in January 2015 submitted a 'proposal for national guidelines for open access to scientific information'. It holds that researchers who receive public grants must either publish their articles in OA journals or upload them to an OA repository after an embargo period of 12 months in educational sciences, humanities and social sciences, and six months in other disciplines.[52]

In *France*, the 'Centre national de la recherche scientifique' (CNRS), the largest fundamental research organization in Europe, has been running the national publication repository 'Hyper Articles en Ligne' (HAL) since 2001, which many research organizations use to build their institutional repositories and which also serves as an archive for PhD theses. The main French funding body, the 'Agence Nationale de la Recherche' (ANR) requires researchers to deposit all publications funded by it in the HAL open archive system 'at the earliest possible opportunity'. However, apart from the social sciences and humanities branch of the ANR, which has provided for an OA mandate since 2007, the French national research funding organizations do not issue a specified OA mandate.

Besides these national policies, the *European Commission* has been involved with open access since 2006.[53] In August 2008, as part of its Seventh Framework Program (FP7), the Commission launched the 'Open Access Pilot', which in special clause 39 requests all grant beneficiaries in the seven eligible research areas to deposit peer-reviewed articles or final manuscripts resulting from their projects in an online repository and to make their best efforts to ensure OA to these articles either six or

---

[52]   www.vr.se/inenglish/researchfunding/applyforgrants/conditionsforapplica tionsandgrants/_openaccess.4.44482f6612355bb5ee780003075.html.
[53]   See the overview at http://ec.europa.eu/research/openscience/index.cfm?pg= openaccess.

12 months after publication, depending on the discipline. Furthermore, general FP7 rules allow for the reimbursement of APCs. In December 2013, the Commission launched 'Horizon 2020', its largest Research and Innovation Programme yet, with nearly €80 billion of funding available from 2014 to 2020. All its beneficiaries must make any peer-reviewed journal article they publish openly accessible free of charge, either via an OA journal (where APCs are eligible for reimbursement), or via an OA repository after an embargo period of six or 12 months.[54] Thus, the Commission has imposed an OA mandate on peer-reviewed scientific publications, which has also triggered corresponding discussions in the EU member states.

2.3.2.2.2 Support by research funders   A number of funders have also introduced OA mandates in order to spread the results of the research they support. A prominent example is the Wellcome Trust, a UK-based charity focusing on health issues, which introduced its OA mandate in 2006. The Trust requires

> electronic copies of any research papers that have been accepted for publication in a peer-reviewed journal, and are supported in whole or in part by Wellcome Trust funding, to be made available through PubMed Central (PMC) and Europe PMC as soon as possible and in any event within six months of the journal publisher's official date of final publication.

Furthermore, it also 'encourages – and where it pays an open access fee, requires – authors and publishers to license research papers using the Creative Commons Attribution license (CC-BY) so they may be freely copied and re-used (for example, for text- and data-mining purposes or creating a translation), provided that such uses are fully attributed. . .'.[55] The US National Institutes of Health (NIH) constitute another example. Already in 2005, they introduced a 'policy on enhancing public access to archived publications resulting from NIH-funded research'.[56] The policy, which was initially voluntary but turned mandatory in 2008, requests all investigators who are in whole or in part funded by the NIH to submit to PubMed Central an electronic version of their final manuscripts upon acceptance for publication as soon as possible and within 12 months of the publisher's official date of final publication.

---

[54]   Furthermore, Horizon 2020 also supports OA to research data and launched the Open Research Data pilot.
[55]   See https://wellcome.ac.uk/funding/managing-grant/open-access-policy.
[56]   See http://grants.nih.gov/grants/guide/notice-files/NOT-OD-05-022.html.

Numerous research funders in various countries follow open access policies of some scope and strength. The European Commission (Archambault et al. 2014: 10) for example counts 34 OA mandates in the UK, 14 in Canada, nine in the US, six in Denmark, five in Ireland and five in France. The major international organizations to conduct and fund research, such as the World Bank, the UNESCO, the European Research Council and the World Health Organization, have also implemented their own policies on free access to their publications which, however, differ not only in the degree of transparency but also in the ways they support open access. Such differences can be categorized along the following characteristics (Archambault et al. 2014: 11): (1) reimbursement of article processing charges; (2) preference for gold versus green OA; (3) the types of documents and metadata that are accepted (e.g. final peer-reviewed manuscript); (4) the threshold beyond which the policy applies regarding the percentage of state funding or the number of authors who are grantees; (5) if the policy supports green OA, the length of the embargo period; (6) the expectations regarding compliance with the policy.

2.3.2.2.3 Support by universities and research institutes Finally, many universities and research institutes have their own open access policies, and some of them are part of international networks to foster open access. To mention only a few prominent examples from Europe (Archambault et al. 2014: 11–13): The University of Southampton (UK) not only hosts the 'Registry of Open Access Repositories' (ROAR) and the 'Registry of Open Access Repository Mandates and Policies' (ROARMAP), but its School of Electronics and Computer Science furthermore adopted an OA mandate as early as 2002. The European Organization for Nuclear Research (CERN, Switzerland) implemented a self-archiving policy already in 2003 and has been encouraging publications in OA journals since 2005. Since 2014, all CERN authors are requested to publish their results under gold OA.[57] This policy has been supported by the establishment of SCOAP³, the 'Sponsoring Consortium for Open Access Publishing in Particle Physics', a global partnership of 3,000 libraries, funding agencies and research institutions from 47 countries and Intergovernmental Organizations.[58] The University of Minho (Portugal) established an institutional repository (RepositóriUM) in 2003 and adopted its OA mandate in 2004. The University of Nottingham (UK) has played a key role in the establishment of OA repositories and since 2002 has been leading the SHERPA

---

[57] http://cds.cern.ch/record/1955574.
[58] https://scoap3.org.

partnership, which operates RoMEO (information about publishers' copyright and archiving policies), JULIET (information on research funders' archiving mandates and guidelines), OpenDOAR (the other global directory of OA repositories besides ROAR), and SHERPA search, a simple full-text search of UK repositories. The university adopted its own OA mandate in 2009. Since July 2015, the Dutch universities have reached several agreements with the publishers SAGE, Elsevier and Wiley regarding open access publishing.

In the US, Harvard University has been hosting the Harvard Open Access Project since 2011. It is led by Peter Suber, one of the world's most prominent advocates for open access. At the core, Harvard's open access policy supports an opt-out solution, which was adopted in 2008 and can be characterized as follows:

> Each Faculty member grants to the President and Fellows of Harvard College permission to make available his or her scholarly articles and to exercise the copyright in those articles. In legal terms, the permission granted by each Faculty member is a nonexclusive, irrevocable, paid-up, worldwide license to exercise any and all rights under copyright relating to each of his or her scholarly articles, in any medium, and to authorize others to do the same, provided that the articles are not sold for a profit.[59]

Cornell University (US) hosts arXiv, which was established in 1991 and is one of the most prominent OA repositories. There is no OA mandate, though the University Faculty Senate in a 2005 resolution strongly encouraged all faculty members to consider publishing in OA.[60]

Furthermore, there are some prominent examples of international cooperation between universities and other relevant players to foster open access. Already in 1997, the São Paulo Research Foundation and the Brazilian National Council for Scientific and Technological Development along with the Latin American and Caribbean Center on Health Sciences Information created SciELO (Scientific Electronic Library Online), which comprises a bibliographic database, a digital library, and a 'cooperative electronic publishing model' of open access journals. Today, the group of participating universities extends beyond most Latin American countries to South Africa, Portugal and Spain. In 2016, 1,249 journals from 14 countries used this platform.[61] A few years later, in 2002, a research project at the

---

[59] https://dash.harvard.edu/bitstream/handle/1/4322574/suber_harvard.html? sequence=1.
[60] https://arxiv.org/help/general.
[61] See Solomon et al. (2016: 137).

Autonomous University of Mexico State produced Redalyc (Network of Scientific Journals from Latin America, the Caribbean, Spain and Portugal), which today provides open and free access to more than 640 journals from the participating countries.[62] In 2012, France, Greece, Italy, Portugal, Spain and Turkey established the 'Mediterranean Open Access Network' (MedOANet) to coordinate their open access policies and in October 2013 issued the 'MedOANet Guidelines for Implementing Open Access Policies for Research Performing and Research Funding Organizations'.[63] Since 2015, the Open Library of Humanities, a non-for-profit publishing platform registered in Cambridge, UK, has been supporting academic journals from the humanities and hosting its own multidisciplinary journal. Publication costs are covered by an international library consortium.[64]

2.4 PRELIMINARY RESULTS

When publishing articles in academic journals, most scholars are predominantly motivated by curiosity, priority and the expected gain in reputation, and much less so by any monetary rewards for the actual publications. While academic journals have been published for several hundred years by non-for-profit organizations, such as learned societies and universities, commercial publishers have been gaining importance since the 1950s. Today the five largest commercial publishers control around 50 percent of the market for academic journals and, in particular, a large share of valuable journals with high impact factors. The growing importance of electronic publishing since the 1990s had two effects. On one hand, it has raised the bargaining power of the publishers vis-à-vis the academic libraries, which has enabled them to increase journal prices and profits and caused the so-called 'serial crisis'. On the other hand, it has induced the victims of the serial crisis, i.e. in particular academic scholars, academic libraries and research sponsors, to look for an alternative to the traditional business model in academic publishing, which had the publishers cover their costs (and feed their profits) from subscription fees. That alternative may be the OA business model, in which all readers with an internet connection have open access to academic articles and the publication costs are covered by author fees and other revenues.

---

[62] See www.unesco.org/new/en/communication-and-information/portals-and-platforms/goap/key-organizations/ latin-america-and-the-caribbean/uaem.
[63] For more details, see Eger et al. (2016).
[64] https://www.openlibhums.org.

This chapter has provided some objective data about the development of OA in academic publishing since the 1990s, including the enormous increase in OA journals (gold OA) since the turn of the century, the differences in publication cultures between the academic disciplines, and some typical differences between CA and OA journals in the different disciplines. Moreover, during the same period, the data also reveal a drastic increase in the importance of disciplinary and institutional repositories and academic social networks (green OA), again with remarkable differences among disciplines. In order to protect their traditional business model based on subscription fees, commercial publishers of original scholarly articles, being the copyright holders, have urged the OA repositories to impose a number of restrictions for uploading the papers and have even acquired some of the repositories. At the same time, scholars, research sponsors, academic libraries and political authorities are engaging in numerous initiatives and projects to foster OA to academic publishing.

In the following chapter, we complement this 'objective' approach with a 'subjective' one, i.e. with the differing perspective on how this development is perceived by the scholarly authors themselves. To that end, we rely on the results of an international survey on authors' perceptions of and attitudes towards open access, which we conducted between September 2012 and December 2015.

3. An international survey analysis

3.1 RESEARCH SETTING

3.1.1 Research Questions

As we have shown before, the number of OA journals and OA repositories has increased dramatically over the last 15 years on a global scale. However, clearly not all countries and disciplines have shared this impressive development to the same degree. While a few of them are enjoying a breakthrough to the new modes of academic publishing, others lag behind. How can these differences be explained? One avenue of investigation is to simply ask the relevant players, i.e. the academic scholars. Are they aware of the two roads to open access? If so, what are their specific incentives to choose OA journals or repositories over the traditional channels of publication? Are there any specific obstacles in the laws or the cultures of the countries concerned? Do the specific reward systems and publication cultures in various disciplines support or impede open access?

To find answers to these questions, in the period 2012 to 2015 we conducted a survey among academic scholars from all disciplines and from 25 countries (one of which is the Benelux group of countries). Being interested in the researchers' experiences with both the gold and green road of OA publishing, we had the questionnaire ask whether a respondent had ever published a paper in an OA journal (OA repository) and, if so, what percentage of their publications of the last five years had been made openly accessible via the gold or the green road. To explain the differences in the scholars' use of open access, we also elicited a number of personal characteristics, including age and professional status, as well as the discipline-specific reward structure and publication culture, and supporting or impeding effects of the legal framework and the general policy towards open access.

More than 10,000 completed questionnaires were returned. They provide the basis of our empirical investigation.

3.1.2 Conducting the Survey

Following a pre-test in all faculties of the University of Hamburg, the first wave of the survey covered Germany.[1] After ten days, the questionnaire was amended slightly to incorporate some feedback by early respondents. We then continued with the (modified) survey in Germany and, successively, with further surveys in 24 additional countries. The surveys started in September 2012 in Germany and finished in December 2015 in Israel (see Table 3.1). The questionnaire was translated into English and into the national languages of the target countries by native speakers who were familiar with the subject matter, and it was then emailed to

Table 3.1   Timing of the surveys

Country	Start	End
Germany	27.09.2012	14.12.2012
India	07.11.2012	03.02.2013
Switzerland	20.12.2012	01.03.2013
Austria	07.01.2013	01.03.2013
Spain	12.03.2013	10.04.2013
Italy	12.04.2013	31.05.2013
Turkey	24.04.2013	31.07.2013
Egypt	26.04.2013	03.12.2013
Brazil	07.05.2013	03.11.2013
France	15.05.2013	31.07.2013
Greece	21.05.2013	11.12.2013
United Kingdom	28.05.2013	31.03.2014
Benelux	19.06.2013	31.07.2013
Finland	24.07.2013	11.12.2013
Poland	28.08.2013	11.12.2013
Hungary	29.08.2013	11.12.2013
Lithuania	15.10.2013	15.04.2014
Slovakia	15.10.2013	15.04.2014
Czech Republic	26.11.2013	15.04.2014
Portugal	12.03.2014	31.05.2014
USA	01.08.2014	31.12.2014
Denmark	10.04.2015	31.07.2015
Sweden	24.04.2015	31.07.2015
Russia	02.06.2015	31.07.2015
Israel	26.10.2015	31.12.2015

[1]   The results are published in Eger et al. (2015).

academic scholars at universities and research institutes. In most continental European countries, the respondents were reached via their heads of faculty or department. In some non-European countries, we collected the email addresses of the researchers from the relevant homepages; in Brazil, we obtained the addresses from the professional associations. For Brazil, Egypt, India, the UK and the US, we found cooperation partners who were explicitly mentioned in the emails in order to increase the response rate. For many other countries, we received more informal support from students and colleagues. The survey results from Bulgaria, China and Ireland are not included in the analysis due to poor response rates.

3.2 DESCRIPTIVE STATISTICS

3.2.1 A General Overview

In total, the survey yielded 10,469 completed questionnaires covering 15 disciplines[2] and 25 countries. Table 3.2 provides an overview of the number of responses by discipline and country. Note that the table and subsequent analysis omit all responses by researchers who indicated that they have no publishing experience (i.e. mostly PhD students).

The highest number of responses was obtained from Germany (1,913), followed by Spain (1,291) and Benelux (727). The most frequently named academic discipline was 'Social Science' (1,416), followed by 'Biology and Life Science' (1,332) and 'Technology and Engineering' (1,166).

With a view to the regression analysis (see chapter 3.3), the information we collected can be categorized into two sets of indicators – dependent and explanatory variables (see Table 3.3). We use four alternative dependent variables. *OA_pub* is a binary variable indicating whether a researcher has at any point published in an OA journal (gold road). *REP_pub* provides the equivalent information with respect to the green road (use of a repository or self-archiving platform). The means of these variables tell us that while more than 50 percent of the respondents have used the gold road of OA, only around 28 percent have at least once deposited their work in a repository or on a self-archiving platform. The two *_degree* variables provide a more fine-grained image of essentially the same information. *OA_degree* ranges from 0 (no use whatsoever of OA journals) to 5 (at least

---

[2]   The discipline categories follow the categorization of the DOAJ (http://doaj. org). For more details see also chapter 2.2.1.1.

Table 3.2 Number of responses by country and discipline

Country	Agri	Art	Bio	Bus	Chem	Earth	Health	Hist	LaPo	Lang	Math	Phil	Phys	Social	Tech	Total
Austria	26	21	88	53	14	43	28	70	46	29	37	20	23	67	113	678
Benelux	25	11	143	28	12	44	94	9	53	27	18	16	41	152	54	727
Brazil	31	5	70	7	8	22	135	6	8	23	7	0	20	27	25	394
Czech Rep.	41	3	45	13	6	12	28	6	12	15	5	3	2	24	20	235
Denmark	20	3	23	8	2	4	73	8	21	37	10	6	6	44	0	265
Egypt	51	1	39	12	26	15	64	1	8	3	16	0	12	8	30	286
Finland	18	9	64	48	24	36	37	9	22	16	23	6	54	51	127	544
France	4	17	33	21	32	25	33	33	20	30	16	9	24	47	36	380
Germany	45	9	303	114	91	156	114	59	100	146	70	59	201	223	222	1,912
Greece	8	1	7	8	3	12	16	3	3	11	2	0	3	15	38	130
Hungary	5	5	27	18	13	25	4	19	29	29	15	11	32	51	78	361
India	2	1	43	29	15	11	12	4	8	19	10	4	20	43	46	267
Israel	0	0	12	0	1	1	29	4	2	3	4	0	0	4	2	62
Italy	18	30	42	52	46	12	37	27	43	54	45	16	28	76	70	596
Lithuania	3	3	12	8	4	2	9	1	14	7	10	0	6	34	45	158
Poland	9	3	16	29	13	3	8	0	19	10	8	0	3	28	25	174
Portugal	3	3	31	4	18	4	23	1	3	7	6	0	6	11	23	143
Russia	0	2	6	9	16	10	5	11	7	38	16	5	17	19	0	161
Slovakia	2	4	6	16	1	8	11	2	11	10	3	3	1	28	10	116
Spain	27	20	115	113	56	66	162	78	94	115	84	19	56	198	88	1,291
Sweden	3	6	13	11	7	13	11	4	1	14	5	3	19	46	19	175
Switzerland	11	9	165	30	17	50	53	37	33	57	20	28	25	85	31	651
Turkey	5	7	5	15	11	5	20	0	3	3	5	1	7	12	32	131
UK	3	11	55	23	4	20	18	10	20	33	9	6	26	70	27	335
USA	1	16	11	18	6	8	27	18	22	49	11	13	15	56	20	291
Total	357	198	1,332	676	444	598	1,050	400	594	771	450	221	641	1,416	11,66	10,469

Table 3.3   Summary statistics

Variable	Obs.	Mean	Std. Dev.	Min	Max
Dependent Variables					
OA_pub	10,469	0.505	0.5	0	1
OA_degree	10,469	1.146	1.428	0	5
REP_pub	10,469	0.278	0.448	0	1
REP_degree	10,469	1.124	0.157	0	5
Explanatory Variables					
Personal and Professional Traits					
years_acad	10,469	17.322	11.505	0	63
professional	10,469	0.833	0.373	0	1
institute	10,469	0.128	0.334	0	1
Inherent Reward System					
j_ranking	10,469	3.173	0.976	0	5
no_publication	10,469	3.052	0.903	0	5
no_monograph	10,469	2.294	1.056	0	5
refereed_j	10,469	3.429	1.038	0	5
Personal Opinions about OA					
OA_readership	10,469	3.171	1.568	0	5
OA_citation	10,469	2.941	1.627	0	5
REP_readership	10,469	2.901	1.654	0	5
REP_citation	10,469	2.725	1.645	0	5
OA_importance	10,469	2.220	1.343	0	5
REP_importance	10,469	1.820	1.363	0	5
OA_quality	10,469	2.894	1.529	0	5
REP_quality	10,469	1.740	1.675	0	5
OA_young	10,469	2.465	1.547	0	5
OA_future	10,469	3.524	1.483	0	5
Assessments of OA per Discipline					
OA_awareness	10,469	3.159	1.414	0	5
OA_relevance	10,469	2.803	1.416	0	5

75 percent of all articles published in an OA journal).[3] Accordingly, *REP_degree* applies to the degree of using the green road.

In turn, our explanatory variables can be differentiated into four categories. The first category comprises personal and professional traits. In this regard, *years_acad* refers to the number of years a respondent has spent in academia since the completion of her PhD, and it ranges from 0

---

[3]   The coding in full: 0 (no experience with OA), 1 (the respondent has provided OA to less than 10 percent of her works over the last five years), 2 (10–25 percent), 3 (25–50 percent), 4 (50–75 percent) and 5 (more than 75 percent).

(no PhD) to 63 years, with an average of around 17 years of post-doctorate experience in academia. The binary variable *professional* indicates whether or not a respondent has a PhD. By this measure, around 83 percent of the respondents are professionals. Finally, in this category, the *institute* dummy equals one if a respondent is affiliated with a research institute, as opposed to a (public) university. The second set of variables characterizes the inherent rewards system, asking how important (0 = utterly unimportant, 5 = very important) to the researcher's career the following achievements are: *ranking*/reputation of the journals published in, number of *publications*, number of *monographs*, and *reviewer* services for journals. A third category of variables captures the respondents' personal opinions about OA: *OA_readership* (*REP_readership*) and *OA_citations* (*REP_citations*) ask whether the respondent agrees that OA journals (repositories/self-arching platforms) yield a wider readership or more citations than a toll access regime, respectively. *OA_importance* (*REP_importance*) and *OA_quality* (*REP_quality*) seek to capture the perceived overall importance and quality of OA journals and repositories, respectively, in the respondent's field of research, with the answer options again ranging from 0 to 5. In addition, *OA_young* asks whether the respondents agree (0 = completely disagree; 5 = completely agree) that OA poses a particular risk for young researchers. Finally, *OA_future* asks the respondents to what extent they agree that OA should be the future of academic publishing. Our fourth set of variables measure how aware the respondents are of OA journals and how relevant they perceive OA journals to be for their careers.

In the following, we provide a detailed overview of the survey results, focusing first on research fields and then on countries, and in each case distinguishing between the gold road and the green road of OA publishing.

3.2.2 By Research Field

3.2.2.1 The gold road
For the gold road of OA publishing (i.e. journals), Figure 3.1 provides a scatter plot of the discipline averages of *OA_pub* and *OA_degree*.[4] Evidently, the gold road to OA is most prevalent in 'Biology and Life Science' (with a mean *OA_degree* of 1.82),[5] where more than 66 percent of all researchers have published at least once in an OA journal. Other

---

[4] For the exact numbers for each field see Table A.3.1 in Appendix 3.
[5] Note that the means include those researchers who have no experience with OA and hence an *OA_degree* of 0.

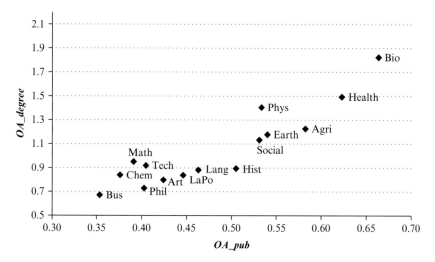

Figure 3.1   Discipline averages of OA_pub *and* OA_degree

disciplines with a high affinity to gold road OA include 'Health Science' (1.49 / 62 percent) and 'Physics and Astronomy' (1.41 / 53 percent). At the bottom end, we have 'Business and Economics' (0.67 / 35 percent).

Furthermore, we asked the respondents for their general assessment (on a 0 to 5 scale) of the *awareness* and *relevance* of OA journals in their discipline. Figure 3.2 sets the discipline average of the relevance factor[6] in relation to the mean of *OA_pub*.

The scatter plot reveals an almost linear positive relationship between the perceived relevance of OA publishing in a field and the share of authors who publish in OA journals. For example, only 35 percent of the respondents from 'Business and Economics' have published in OA journals and, at 2.28, this discipline also features the second lowest level of relevance. At the other end, 'Biology and Life Science' is the discipline with both the largest share of OA-experienced researchers (66 percent) and the highest perceived relevance (3.39). A very similar picture of a strong positive relationship emerges if we replace the relevance factor with the values for awareness,[7] which is to be expected, given the strong correlation between the indicators for relevance and awareness (r = 0.64).

---

6   For the detailed numbers see Table A.3.2 in Appendix 3.
7   See Figure A.3.1 in Appendix 3.

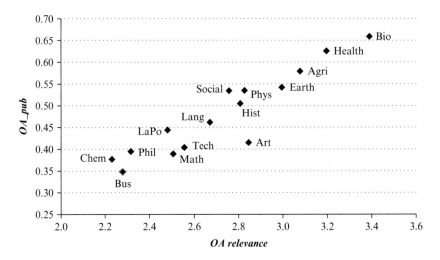

Figure 3.2   Discipline averages of OA relevance *and* OA_pub

3.2.2.2   The green road

With respect to the green road (self-archiving or online repositories) of OA publishing, we find similar 'cultural paths' in the experiences with and the attitude towards self-archiving or online repositories by discipline. Figure 3.3 shows the relationship between the average usage rates (*REP_pub*) per discipline and the extent to which researchers provide free online access to their works by using self-archiving platforms or repositories.

The figure shows that respondents from 'Chemistry', 'Health Science' and 'Biology and Life Science' use the green road the least, both in terms of average usage rates in general and in terms of the degree of research material that is available via such online platforms. By contrast, we find that self-archiving of research papers is most common in 'Physics and Astronomy', 'Mathematics and Statistics' and, to a lesser extent, also in 'Business and Economics'. In terms of general usage rates, we observe that more than 60 percent of all researchers in 'Physics and Astronomy' use the green road, followed by around 56 percent of the respondents from 'Mathematics and Statistics' and more than 40 percent from 'Business and Economics'. This is interesting in that previously we saw that these disciplines exhibit very low usage rates for the gold road of OA publishing. In terms of the *degree* of green road usage, respondents from 'Mathematics and Statistics' and 'Physics and Astronomy' exhibit an average of around 2, while those from 'Business and Economics' feature an average of almost 1.4.

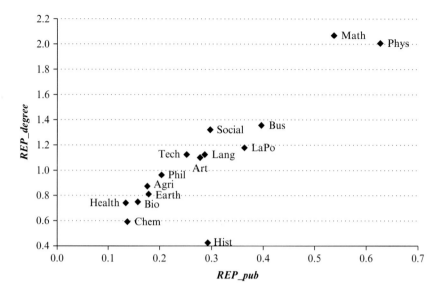

Figure 3.3   Discipline averages of REP_pub *and* REP_degree

Not surprisingly, these differences in the use of the green road appear to be related to the perceived importance of repositories in the respondents' fields. Figure 3.4 displays this relationship by means of the discipline averages of *REP_importance* and *REP_pub*.

We find that the greater the perceived importance of the green road in a field of research, the more green-road-experience the respondents in this field tend to have. However, this relationship is not quite as pronounced as the one we saw previously between relevance and *OA_pub* in the context of the gold road. For example, 'Business and Economics' features a relatively large share of scholars who have already uploaded at least one paper in a repository (41 percent, ranking third after physics and mathematics), whereas the perceived importance of repositories in this discipline is relatively low (1.45).

3.2.2.3   Conclusions

Importantly, a discipline that exhibits an affinity to one road to OA may or may not also embrace the other road. For example, we observe high usage rates of the gold road in some disciplines (especially 'Biology and Life Science' and 'Health Sciences') where, however, little use is made of the green road. Conversely, a number of other disciplines (especially 'Physics and Astronomy' and 'Mathematics and Statistics') exhibit the opposite tendency. Figure 3.5 displays the discipline-average usage rates

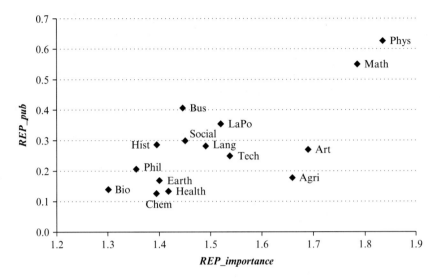

Figure 3.4   Discipline averages of REP_importance *and* REP_pub

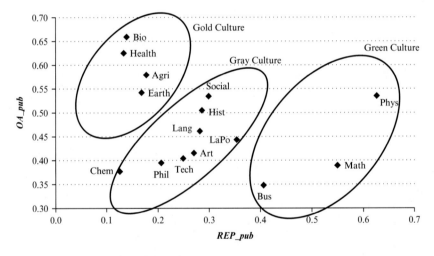

Figure 3.5   OA publishing cultures

of the gold versus the green road.[8] It shows no systematic tendency for the disciplines to simultaneously embrace both roads, or neither. If anything,

---

[8]   Note that a similar picture emerges if the 'pub' variables are replaced by the respective 'degree' indicators.

if we were to discard 'Physics and Astronomy' and 'Chemistry', a negative relationship might be detected, suggesting that the two roads are perceived as substitutes for each other, i.e. a discipline tends to lean *either* towards the gold road or towards the green road.

This image suggests that three different publishing cultures might be distinguished: (1) The *gold culture* ('Biology and Life Science', 'Health Science', 'Agricultural Science' and 'Earth and Environmental Science') with high usage rates for OA journals but little use of online repositories or self-archiving platforms; the *green culture* ('Physics and Astronomy', 'Mathematics and Statistics' and 'Business and Economics') with little use of OA journals but strong use of repositories and other online platforms, and a *gray culture* (e.g. 'Social Sciences', 'Technology and Engineering' and 'Chemistry') with mediocre use of both roads.[9]

3.2.3 By Country

Following the analysis in terms of disciplines, we now consider any geographical variation in the use of gold and green road OA publishing. The data set comprises researchers from 25 countries, 17 of which are part of the European Union.[10] Furthermore, the sample comprises four countries that are commonly considered emerging market economies: Brazil, Russia, India and Egypt.

3.2.3.1 The gold road
In Figure 3.6, we see a relatively clear positive relationship between the usage rate and the degree of publications in OA journals in the 25 countries. While 80 percent of the respondents from the Benelux countries have published in OA journals, with an average degree of 1.78, at the other extreme, only 27 percent of the Slovakia-based respondents have done so, with an average degree of 0.54.

We may again ask whether there is any association between the actual use of OA journals (*OA_pub*) and their perceived relevance, though this time we average across countries rather than disciplines. In this sense, Figure 3.7 below is the mirror image of Figure 3.2 above.

Most strikingly, in contrast to the corresponding image for the discipline averages (Figure 3.2), here we see no clear relationship between the

---

[9] Note that this delineation of cultures does not coincide with the four research fields we have used in chapter 2.

[10] Note that Benelux (Belgium, the Netherlands and Luxembourg) is considered one country as we collected the data from this area in a single survey round. Moreover, the UK is counted 'in' as the survey was conducted pre-Brexit.

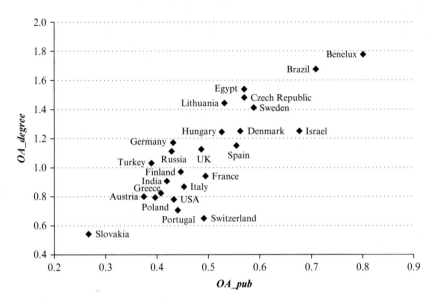

Figure 3.6   Country averages of OA_pub *and* OA_degree

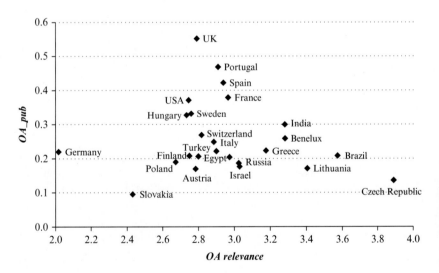

Figure 3.7   Country averages for OA_pub *and* OA relevance

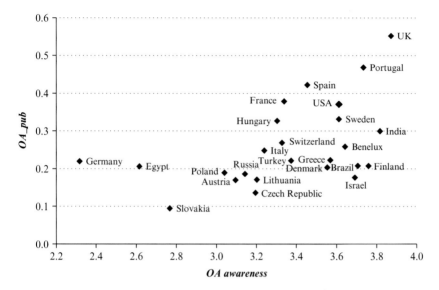

Figure 3.8   Country averages for OA_pub *and* OA awareness

relevance of OA journals and the respondents' actual use of the gold road: OA journals are used most widely in the UK, followed by Portugal, Spain and France, while they are perceived to be only of average relevance in these countries.[11] Conversely, OA journals are considered most relevant by respondents from the Czech Republic, while these researchers have the second least experience with this publishing regime.

In Figure 3.8 above, we replace *relevance* with *awareness* of OA journals and obtain a somewhat clearer relationship.

There does seem to be a slight positive association, on a cross-country basis, between OA journal publishing experience and the awareness of that avenue. Both variables are highest for the UK. By contrast, Germany has the lowest awareness factor and ranges in the lower third with respect to OA journal usage. Again, it seems that variations in publishing culture are determined mostly by the respondents' field of research and much less so by geography.

---

[11]   This does not quite match the ordering of countries with respect to the numbers of OA journals, as reported in Table 2.7 in chapter 2: 1. Brazil, 2. UK, 3. US, 4. Egypt, 5. Spain . . . There are two possible reasons for this discrepancy: (1) While Table 2.8 refers to the country of residence of the *publisher* of the OA journal, Figures 3.6–3.8 indicate the country of the *scholar* who published articles in an OA journal. (2) There are large differences among the *response rates* from different countries.

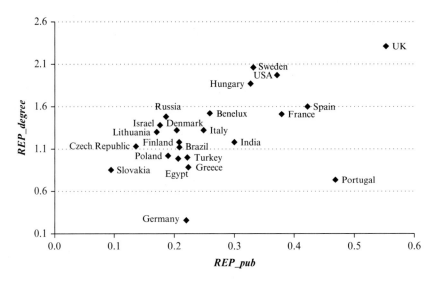

Figure 3.9   Country averages of REP_pub *and* REP_degree

3.2.3.2   The green road

With respect to the green road (self-archiving or online repositories) of OA publishing, we find similar 'cultural paths' in the experiences with and the attitude towards self-archiving or online repositories by country. However, in comparison to our observations by discipline, the relationship seems to be less clear. In this regard, Figure 3.9 shows the 25 country averages for *REP_pub* and *REP_degree*. There is a weak positive relationship between the two indicators. Interestingly, the green road is most prevalent, by both measures, in the UK. Almost 60 percent of the UK-based respondents have already deposited works online, with an average degree of 2.3. Thus, on average, more than a quarter of the works that the respondents published in the last five years are available online. Trailing far behind the UK are Spain, Sweden, the USA, France and Hungary. Very low usage rates are found in Slovakia and the Czech Republic. At the bottom end in terms of *REP_degree*, respondents from Germany only provide green road open access to well below 10 percent of their recent research.

Looking at the perceived importance of green OA publishing by country (Figure 3.10), our findings are not as clear-cut as with the discipline-specific picture. While we find the highest usage rates (*REP_pub*) in the UK, Portugal and Spain, respondents from these countries attribute only average importance to this form of OA publishing.

Indeed, the extreme case of Egypt suggests the very opposite. While

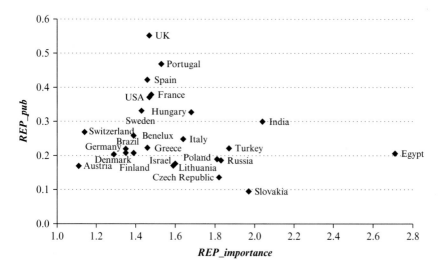

Figure 3.10   Country averages of REP_pub *and* REP_importance

respondents from Egypt perceive online repositories to be extremely important, their usage rates rank among the lower third. It thus appears that the reasons for researchers to provide green OA to their works are less driven by their country of residence.

3.2.3.3   Conclusions

All of the above suggests that the publishing culture and hence the attitude towards both roads of OA is more likely to be driven by the respondents' field of research than by their country of residence. Figure 3.11 summarizes the country averages for both roads to OA, using *OA_pub* and *REP_pub* as reference variables. Comparing Figure 3.11 to what we saw when looking at the usage of both OA regimes by discipline (Figure 3.5) suggests that publishing culture is unlikely to be a national phenomenon.

To mention only a few examples, we find that 80 percent of the respondents from Benelux have experience with depositing their works in online repositories of some form, while only around 26 percent of them have published in an OA journal. OA journals are most popular among respondents from the UK, followed by Portugal, Spain and France. Generally, geography does not seem to matter to the attitudes towards both roads of OA publishing.

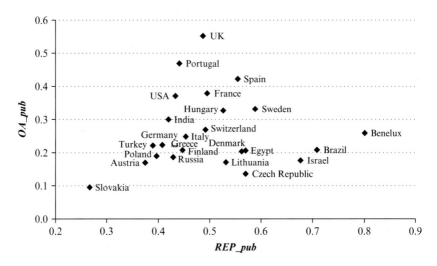

Figure 3.11   Country averages of OA_pub *and* REP_pub

3.3   EMPIRICAL ANALYSIS

3.3.1   Method

Recall that the motivation for our international survey was to explain differences in OA publishing among disciplines and countries. Are scholars aware of the two roads to open access? If so, what are their specific incentives to choose OA journals or repositories over the traditional channels of publication? Are there any specific obstacles in the laws or the cultures of the countries concerned? Do the specific reward systems and publication cultures in various disciplines support or impede open access? For that reason, in the following we run a number of regressions aiming to explain two alternative dependent variables, which result from the answers to the following two questions: 'Have you ever published a paper in an OA journal?' and 'Have you ever deposited a work on a self-archiving platform or repository?'[12] We chose the two binary variables *OA_pub* and *REP_pub*, rather than the more fine-grained degree variants, for the sake of simplicity. This is justified because, at least with respect to disciplines, there is a strong positive correlation between the binary and the degree variable for both roads to OA (see Figures 3.1 and 3.3). To examine how a

---

[12]   Please find the complete questionnaire below, in Appendix 4.

set of explanatory variables affect the probability of the respective positive outcome occurring, we use a logit regression model of the following type (Long and Freese 2014, chapters 5 and 6):

$$y_i = \alpha + \beta X_i' + e_i,$$

where y denotes either of the two binary dependent variables, X' is a vector representing a combination of explanatory variables of the four types introduced above (personal and professional traits, inherent reward structure, personal opinion about OA, discipline-average OA assessment), varying with the exact model specification, and α, β and e are the constant, the vector of regression coefficients and the error term, respectively. In light of the systematic differences in OA journal and repository publishing behavior across different disciplines, but to some extent also across countries, we add two sets of dummy variables to control for discipline-specific and country-specific effects. Finally, we use heteroskedasticity-consistent (robust) standard errors.

We run four types of regression models for each road, beginning with the gold road. The basic regression models (Tables 3.4 and 3.8) use the four types of explanatory variables, supplemented by discipline dummies and country dummies. Next, the specific regression models (Tables 3.5 and 3.9) replace the discipline dummies by publishing culture dummies (gold and green culture, with gray culture acting as a reference) and the country dummies by regional dummies (west, east, south and emerging market economies, with the US as the omitted category). Finally, in the last two types of regression models, we investigate the role of the publishing culture in more detail by using as the dependent variable the interaction between cultural membership (gold versus green) and the respective OA binary variable, and we determine the impact of the four groups of explanatory variables on these newly created four dependent variables (Tables 3.6, 3.7, 3.10 and 3.11):

$$z * y_i = \alpha + \beta X_i' + e_i,$$

where z is a dummy for the respondent's publishing culture.

3.3.2 The Gold Road

Our binary logit estimates for the gold road of OA are reported in Table 3.4. Specifications (1) to (3) consider personal and professional traits of the respondents, as well as aspects of the inherent reward system and personal opinions about OA. In specifications (4) to (6), the variables

Table 3.4 Basic regression models on the gold road of OA

Variables	(1)	(2)	(3)	(4)	(5)	(6)
years_acad*	0.0123***	0.0150***	0.0756***	0.0130***	0.0131***	0.0106***
	(0.00209)	(0.00219)	(0.00743)	(0.00226)	(0.00225)	(0.00221)
years_acad^2			-0.00136***			
			(0.000158)			
professional	0.904***	0.963***	0.727***	0.930***	0.930***	0.906***
	(0.0680)	(0.0705)	(0.0756)	(0.0721)	(0.0721)	(0.0715)
institute		0.0832	0.0915	-0.194***	-0.193***	-0.208***
		(0.0683)	(0.0686)	(0.0704)	(0.0704)	(0.0697)
no_publication	0.0256	0.0317	0.0330	0.0225	0.0226	0.0249
	(0.0312)	(0.0327)	(0.0328)	(0.0338)	(0.0338)	(0.0332)
no_monograph	-0.00424	-0.0353	-0.0366	-0.0149	-0.0143	0.00385
	(0.0229)	(0.0239)	(0.0241)	(0.0249)	(0.0249)	(0.0247)
refereed_j	-0.0574	-0.0835*	-0.0892**	-0.167***	-0.168***	-0.161***
	(0.0428)	(0.0453)	(0.0454)	(0.0475)	(0.0475)	(0.0458)
j_ranking	0.0427	0.0464	0.0464	0.00210	0.00228	0.00567
	(0.0321)	(0.0334)	(0.0336)	(0.0346)	(0.0346)	(0.0341)
oa_importance		0.156***	0.160***			
		(0.0202)	(0.0202)			
oa_quality		0.215***	0.214***			
		(0.0170)	(0.0170)			
oa_future		-0.0359*	-0.0351*	-0.0168		
		(0.0192)	(0.0193)	(0.0187)		
oa_readership		0.160***	0.163***	0.176***	0.170***	
		(0.0214)	(0.0215)	(0.0217)	(0.0211)	

	(1)	(2)	(3)	(4)	(5)	(6)
oa_citation		0.0407**	0.0410**	0.0529***	0.0511***	
		(0.0192)	(0.0193)	(0.0195)	(0.0194)	
awareness				0.417***	0.415***	0.433***
				(0.0229)	(0.0228)	(0.0227)
relevance				0.176***	0.174***	0.223***
				(0.0221)	(0.0220)	(0.0213)
Discipline dummies	YES	YES	YES	YES	YES	YES
Country dummies	YES	YES	YES	YES	YES	YES
Observations	10,468	10,468	10,468	10,468	10,468	10,468
Pseudo R^2	0.084	0.136	0.141	0.176	0.176	0.163

Notes: Robust standard errors in parentheses. Constant not reported. *** $p<0.01$, ** $p<0.05$, * $p<0.1$

regarding personal opinions about OA are successively replaced with the discipline-averages regarding the awareness and relevance of OA within the respondents' field of research. Here and in the following we will structure our observations along the four types of models, i.e. the basic models, the specific models, and the two types of models that consider the interaction with the two cultures.

Personal and Professional Traits. The results reveal that publishing in OA journals is related to seniority in a non-linear fashion. In fact, the negative coefficient for *years_acad^2* suggests an inverted u-shaped graph for the likelihood of publishing in OA outlets as a function of seniority: As experience in academia grows, the likelihood of publishing in OA journals initially rises, reaching a maximum at around 28 years,[13] which corresponds to an age of about 53 years if we assume that researchers enter academia at 25. Beyond that point, the likelihood of choosing an OA outlet begins to decline. This may be due either to older researchers' lower affinity towards digitization and hence the OA regime or to their depending less on the perceived quality of publication venues. Next, we find a significant and positive impact of 'being a *professional*' (having a PhD) for all six specifications reported in Table 3.4: Professional status strongly increases the likelihood of using OA journals, with a coefficient of around 0.9 in all but one specification. However, this need not mean that authors with a PhD have a stronger preference for gold OA than those without a PhD. Rather, authors who have progressed further in their academic career will generally have published more, raising the probability of at least one OA publication. Moreover, the inherent reward system may impede OA publications in particular for younger academics who are working towards a tenured position. Moving along, the variable *institute* captures whether a respondent works for a university (0) or research institute (1). In three model specifications, we find a significant negative impact of being with a research institute on the likelihood to publish in an OA journal. A possible explanation is that 'institute' researchers tend to focus even more on research and hence publishing than their peers at universities, and thus consider publications in highly ranked journals to be even more important for their careers (see also the next point).

Inherent Reward System. As we have argued in chapter 2, the inherent reward system in academia is likely to be a driver of the observed differences in usage rates of the gold road across disciplines. Accordingly, we

---

[13]   In Table 3.4, model 3, the impact of 'years in academia' on the usage rate of the gold road is given by $y = 0.0756x - 0.00136x^2 + c$, which reaches its maximum at $x^* = 27.79$.

find examples of disciplines – such as economics and most of sciences – where publications in refereed and highly ranked international journals may most likely boost career chances of researchers. In specifications (3) to (6), we indeed find a negative and significant impact of the perceived relevance of *refereed journal* articles in one's discipline on the likelihood of publishing in OA journals. Recall from chapter 2 that in a number of disciplines, established closed access journals benefit from an impact factor and hence a reputation advantage over (newly established) OA journals. Thus, the credit received from the journal (publisher) may be more important for the decision of the outlet as the mode – i.e. whether the journal follows a closed or open access philosophy.

Personal Opinions about OA. The respondents' personal opinions about OA, which we capture in a total of four variables, are also likely to drive their decisions to publish OA. Table 3.4 shows that all four aspects in fact influence the respondents' likelihood to publish OA. Not surprisingly, we see positive coefficients on both the perceived *importance* and *quality* of OA journals. Most interestingly, respondents who associate OA journals with wider *readership* and, to a weaker extent, with a higher *citation* rate are more likely to publish in OA journals.[14] The greater the perceived readership (and citation) advantage of OA journals over CA journals, the more readily a researcher will submit to an OA journal. Finally, the pseudo R^2 confirms that adding information on the respondents' personal opinions greatly improves the explanatory power of our model.

Assessment of OA per Discipline. To further refine our model, we derive two additional explanatory variables that reflect how OA journals fare in the authors' opinion in a specific field of research. To avoid any problems of collinearity, we dropped the individual opinions about the importance and quality of OA journals from these specifications and included only the discipline-average opinions regarding two questions: First, how *aware* the respondents are of the concept of open access journals. Not surprisingly, greater awareness of OA strongly increases the likelihood to publish in such outlets. Second, we asked how *relevant* the respondents considered OA journals to be in their discipline. In accordance with our findings of an impact factor advantage of established CA journals over OA journals (chapter 2.3.1.1, Table 2.9) in many but not all disciplines, we find that relevance also has a strongly significant and positive impact on the

---

[14] Shavell (2010) argues that readership for OA journals is likely to be (somewhat) higher simply due to the freedom of access to the journal content. However, the literature on the citation advantage of OA over CA reveals a more differentiated picture (see the literature cited in Mueller-Langer and Scheufen (2013)).

likelihood of choosing OA. Note that the awareness factor seems to be more important, as its coefficient is in all specifications larger than that of the relevance factor. This difference may be due to the fact that the (dis)-advantage of OA compared to CA varies considerably across the fields of research. While 'Biology and Life Science' features OA journals such as *PLOS Biology* whose impact factors match those of comparable CA journals, in Economics, for example, the impact factor advantage of CA journals remains quite pronounced.[15] While the regressions in Table 3.4 include a total of 40 discipline and country dummies for all six specifications, they are not reported for reasons of clarity.

Looking at different publishing cultures by discipline necessitates a thorough investigation of the rewards of OA publishing for a researcher's career. We dealt with this question in section 3.2, when we identified three different OA publishing cultures by plotting the means of *OA_pub* and *REP_pub* (see Figure 3.5). We use these definitions to empirically test whether being part of one of these cultures influences the likelihood to embrace OA publishing.

Table 3.5 shows the results of our binary logit estimates, incorporating gold and green culture dummies throughout specifications (2) to (7), with the gray culture serving as a benchmark. Moreover, the table also includes regional dummies instead of separate country dummies.[16] We structure our analysis along the four groups of explanatory variables – personal and professional traits, inherent reward system, personal opinions about OA and assessment of OA per discipline – with the discussion on discipline-specific cultures in OA publishing subsumed under the last group. Note that specification (1) acts as a reference model as it does not yet include the culture dummies. Again, we use the respondents' personal opinions on OA throughout specifications (1) to (4), while the personal assessment is successively replaced by the awareness and relevance factors in specifications (5) to (7).

Personal and Professional Traits. In line with the results of Table 3.4, we find a non-linear influence of seniority on the likelihood of publishing in OA journals. As above, more *years in academia* raise the likelihood of using the gold road up to a maximum at around 28 years after entering academia, beyond which point the influence turns negative. Again, having

---

[15]   Regarding the low standing of OA journals in Economics, see also the survey by Migheli and Ramello (2014).

[16]   The regions are defined as follows: west = Austria, Benelux, France, Germany, Switzerland, UK, Finland, Sweden and Denmark; east = Czech Republic, Poland, Hungary, Slovakia and Lithuania; south = Spain, Italy, Greece, Portugal and Turkey; emerg = India, Egypt, Brazil and Russia. The USA constitute the reference category.

Table 3.5 Specific regression models regarding the gold road of OA

Variables	(1)	(2)	(3)	(4)	(5)	(6)	(7)
years_acad	0.0116***	0.0137***	0.0669***	0.0137***	0.0124***	0.0126***	0.00969***
	(0.00204)	(0.00212)	(0.00717)	(0.00212)	(0.00217)	(0.00217)	(0.00213)
years_acad^2			-0.0012***				
			(0.000153)				
professional	0.794***	0.827***	0.614***	0.827***	0.785***	0.785***	0.770***
	(0.0634)	(0.0655)	(0.0709)	(0.0655)	(0.0672)	(0.0672)	(0.0667)
institute	0.0386		0.00489	-0.00164	-0.156**	-0.155**	-0.141**
	(0.0630)		(0.0649)	(0.0648)	(0.0659)	(0.0659)	(0.0648)
no_publication	-0.0296	-0.0108	-0.0109	-0.0108	-0.0346	-0.0335	-0.0356
	(0.0294)	(0.0307)	(0.0308)	(0.0307)	(0.0318)	(0.0319)	(0.0311)
no_monograph	-0.037*	-0.062***	-0.063***	-0.062***	-0.061***	-0.060***	-0.036
	(0.0219)	(0.0216)	(0.0217)	(0.0216)	(0.0225)	(0.0224)	(0.0221)
refereed_j	0.0681*	0.0392	0.0417	0.0393	0.0668	0.0657	0.0652*
	(0.0361)	(0.0380)	(0.0384)	(0.0381)	(0.0408)	(0.0408)	(0.0394)
j_ranking	0.0186	0.0315	0.0324	0.0315	-0.0136	-0.0125	-0.0163
	(0.0293)	(0.0304)	(0.0305)	(0.0304)	(0.0316)	(0.0316)	(0.0310)
oa_importance		0.151***	0.154***	0.151***			
		(0.0194)	(0.0194)	(0.0194)			
oa_quality		0.235***	0.234***	0.235***			
		(0.0165)	(0.0165)	(0.0165)			
oa_future		-0.0361**	-0.0367**	-0.0361**	-0.0255		
		(0.0184)	(0.0184)	(0.0184)	(0.0178)		
oa_readership		0.154***	0.157***	0.154***	0.190***	0.182***	
		(0.0207)	(0.0208)	(0.0207)	(0.0210)	(0.0205)	
oa_citation		0.0311*	0.0308*	0.0311*	0.0469**	0.0443**	
		(0.0186)	(0.0187)	(0.0186)	(0.0190)	(0.0189)	

Table 3.5   (continued)

Variables	(1)	(2)	(3)	(4)	(5)	(6)	(7)
awareness					0.382***	0.379***	0.385***
					(0.0217)	(0.0216)	(0.0216)
relevance					0.201***	0.199***	0.251***
					(0.0210)	(0.0210)	(0.0203)
west	0.341***	0.233**	0.211*	0.233**	0.488***	0.487***	0.573***
	(0.114)	(0.115)	(0.116)	(0.115)	(0.113)	(0.113)	(0.111)
east	0.284**	0.0161	0.0180	0.0163	0.158	0.165	0.334***
	(0.128)	(0.130)	(0.130)	(0.130)	(0.129)	(0.129)	(0.126)
south	0.236**	−0.0263	−0.0684	−0.0263	0.0658	0.0676	0.231**
	(0.118)	(0.120)	(0.120)	(0.120)	(0.117)	(0.117)	(0.114)
emerg	0.407***	0.152	0.130	0.152	0.321**	0.332**	0.397***
	(0.129)	(0.133)	(0.133)	(0.133)	(0.132)	(0.132)	(0.128)
green		−0.116*	−0.107*	−0.115*	−0.105*	−0.106*	−0.145**
		(0.0597)	(0.0599)	(0.0597)	(0.0620)	(0.0620)	(0.0611)
gold		0.478***	0.467***	0.478***	0.420***	0.420***	0.416***
		(0.0507)	(0.0510)	(0.0509)	(0.0528)	(0.0528)	(0.0520)
Discipline dummies	YES	NO	NO	NO	NO	NO	NO
Country dummies	NO	NO	NO	NO	NO	NO	NO
Observations	10,468	10,468	10,468	10,468	10,468	10,468	10,468
Pseudo R²	0.052	0.099	0.099	0.103	0.144	0.143	0.128

Notes: Robust standard errors in parentheses. Constant not reported. *** $p<0.01$, ** $p<0.05$, * $p<0.1$.

a PhD has a significant and positive impact on the likelihood of gold OA. Moreover, we also find a negative effect of working at a *research institute* for specifications (5) to (7), which accords with the results in Table 3.4.

Inherent Reward Structure. In contrast to the findings reported in Table 3.4, we find little impact of the importance of publications in *refereed journals* on the likelihood of publishing in OA journals. Perhaps the earlier negative impact is now absorbed by the publication cultures, i.e. the discipline-specific effects (see below). We will see that the reward structure and hence the importance of refereed journals differs considerably between disciplines.[17]

Personal opinion about OA. The results confirm that the more *importance* researchers attach to OA publishing, the more likely they are to publish in OA journals. The same relationship holds for the perceived *quality* of OA journals. We also again find that the decision regarding the publication outlet is likewise driven by the *readership* advantage and a considerably weaker *citation* advantage of OA journals.

Assessment of OA per Publishing Culture and Region. Again, we find that the *awareness* and *relevance* of OA journals are good predictors of the publishing decision. Regarding the *country effect*, we find that living in the 'west' increases the likelihood of using the gold road of OA. Being a researcher from an emerging market economy also has a significant and positive impact on the usage rate. This is insofar not surprising as, first, in the ranking of countries that host the most OA journals, Brazil stands at number one, Egypt at four, India at nine and Russia at 16 (see Table 2.7), and second, authors from these countries receive financial support from specific sponsoring programs and from OA publishers of the developed world. Regarding *discipline-specific* or cultural traits, throughout specifications (2) to (7) we find a robust, positive and strongly significant impact of the 'gold culture' on the decision to publish in OA journals, which in a sense is trivial and only confirms our classification of disciplines.

Again, adding information on the respondents' personal opinions about publishing in OA journals and adding the awareness and relevance factors improves the explanatory power of our model.

Tables 3.6 and 3.7 report the results of a more in-depth examination of the role of the publishing culture (green versus gold). Here, as the dependent variable in our empirical model, we use the interaction between cultural membership and the OA binary variable. We begin with the gold

---

[17]   We will highlight *PLOS Biology* as a best practice example of successful OA journals in chapter 4.

Table 3.6 Gold road regression results for the interaction with the gold OA culture

Variables	(1)	(2)	(3)	(4)	(5)	(6)
years_acad	0.0133***	0.0136***	0.0740***	0.0109***	0.0111***	0.00988***
	(0.00245)	(0.00245)	(0.00938)	(0.00247)	(0.00246)	(0.00244)
years_acad^2			-0.00134***			
			(0.000202)			
professional	0.686***	0.685***	0.442***	0.667***	0.666***	0.661***
	(0.0895)	(0.0895)	(0.0967)	(0.0903)	(0.0903)	(0.0899)
institute		0.243***	0.254***	0.135*	0.135*	0.143*
		(0.0718)	(0.0721)	(0.0733)	(0.0734)	(0.0731)
no_publication	0.207***	0.205***	0.207***	0.184***	0.185***	0.181***
	(0.0385)	(0.0385)	(0.0384)	(0.0386)	(0.0386)	(0.0384)
no_monograph	-0.446***	-0.441***	-0.442***	-0.430***	-0.429***	-0.412***
	(0.0253)	(0.0253)	(0.0255)	(0.0258)	(0.0258)	(0.0254)
refereed_j	0.298***	0.289***	0.291***	0.316***	0.316***	0.313***
	(0.0582)	(0.0581)	(0.0578)	(0.0590)	(0.0590)	(0.0585)
j_ranking	0.176***	0.179***	0.179***	0.155***	0.157***	0.149***
	(0.0391)	(0.0392)	(0.0392)	(0.0395)	(0.0395)	(0.0391)
oa_importance	0.163***	0.163***	0.166***			
	(0.0224)	(0.0224)	(0.0225)			
oa_quality	0.235***	0.233***	0.231***			
	(0.0217)	(0.0218)	(0.0218)			
oa_future	-0.0553**	-0.0552**	-0.0553**	-0.0399*		
	(0.0234)	(0.0234)	(0.0235)	(0.0228)		
oa_readership	0.139***	0.137***	0.140***	0.154***	0.142***	
	(0.0265)	(0.0266)	(0.0266)	(0.0267)	(0.0259)	

oa_citation	−0.0213	−0.0206	−0.0208	−0.0136	−0.0171	
	(0.0234)	(0.0235)	(0.0236)	(0.0234)	(0.0233)	
awareness				0.178***	0.173***	0.185***
				(0.0280)	(0.0276)	(0.0276)
relevance				0.375***	0.371***	0.405***
				(0.0266)	(0.0264)	(0.0257)
west	0.387***	0.358**	0.330**	0.490***	0.485***	0.541***
	(0.149)	(0.149)	(0.149)	(0.148)	(0.149)	(0.147)
east	0.161	0.135	0.135	0.132	0.139	0.227
	(0.170)	(0.170)	(0.170)	(0.170)	(0.170)	(0.168)
south	−0.0515	−0.0589	−0.109	−0.0210	−0.0210	0.0654
	(0.157)	(0.157)	(0.157)	(0.156)	(0.156)	(0.154)
emerg	1.087***	1.067***	1.045***	1.164***	1.180***	1.203***
	(0.165)	(0.165)	(0.165)	(0.164)	(0.164)	(0.162)
Observations	10,468	10,468	10,468	10,468	10,468	10,468
Pseudo R^2	0.103	0.104	0.109	0.133	0.133	0.128

Notes: Robust standard errors in parentheses. Constant not reported. *** $p<0.01$, ** $p<0.05$, * $p<0.1$.

83

Table 3.7 Gold road regression results for the interaction with the green OA culture

Variables	(1)	(2)	(3)	(4)	(5)	(6)
years_acad	0.00879**	0.00914**	0.0103	0.00902**	0.00883**	0.00845**
	(0.00367)	(0.00366)	(0.0125)	(0.00370)	(0.00369)	(0.00368)
years_acad^2			−2.44e−05			
			(0.000273)			
professional	0.478***	0.475***	0.470***	0.423***	0.422***	0.420***
	(0.128)	(0.128)	(0.135)	(0.128)	(0.128)	(0.128)
institute		0.258**	0.259**	0.207*	0.207*	0.208**
		(0.106)	(0.106)	(0.106)	(0.106)	(0.106)
no_publication	−0.150***	−0.153***	−0.153***	−0.161***	−0.161***	−0.165***
	(0.0510)	(0.0511)	(0.0511)	(0.0508)	(0.0508)	(0.0508)
no_monograph	−0.281***	−0.274***	−0.274***	−0.268***	−0.269***	−0.267***
	(0.0370)	(0.0374)	(0.0374)	(0.0375)	(0.0373)	(0.0372)
refereed_j	0.130*	0.123*	0.123*	0.119*	0.120*	0.122*
	(0.0703)	(0.0704)	(0.0704)	(0.0704)	(0.0703)	(0.0702)
j_ranking	0.149***	0.151***	0.151***	0.133**	0.131**	0.128**
	(0.0524)	(0.0525)	(0.0525)	(0.0522)	(0.0521)	(0.0521)
oa_importance	0.109***	0.109***	0.109***			
	(0.0318)	(0.0319)	(0.0319)			
oa_quality	0.0334	0.0309	0.0308			
	(0.0295)	(0.0295)	(0.0296)			
oa_future	0.0420	0.0420	0.0420	0.0317		
	(0.0334)	(0.0335)	(0.0335)	(0.0324)		
oa_readership	0.0531	0.0524	0.0524	0.0606*	0.0703**	
	(0.0360)	(0.0362)	(0.0362)	(0.0356)	(0.0343)	

oa_citation	−0.0503	−0.0498	−0.0498	−0.0442	−0.0417	0.00335
	(0.0312)	(0.0313)	(0.0313)	(0.0306)	(0.0307)	(0.0229)
awareness				0.203***	0.208***	0.209***
				(0.0375)	(0.0371)	(0.0372)
relevance				−0.00396	−0.00166	0.00585
				(0.0364)	(0.0364)	(0.0361)
west	0.615**	0.583**	0.582**	0.664**	0.667**	0.690***
	(0.258)	(0.258)	(0.258)	(0.259)	(0.259)	(0.259)
east	0.531*	0.500*	0.500*	0.604**	0.598**	0.620**
	(0.282)	(0.282)	(0.282)	(0.284)	(0.284)	(0.284)
south	0.500*	0.492*	0.491*	0.543**	0.542**	0.568**
	(0.264)	(0.264)	(0.263)	(0.265)	(0.265)	(0.265)
emerg	0.551**	0.530*	0.530*	0.664**	0.651**	0.657**
	(0.278)	(0.278)	(0.278)	(0.280)	(0.280)	(0.280)
Observations	10,468	10,468	10,468	10,468	10,468	10,468
Pseudo R²	0.026	0.028	0.028	0.034	0.033	0.033

Notes: Robust standard errors in parentheses. Constant not reported. *** p<0.01, ** p<0.05, * p<0.1

culture interaction term (Table 3.6), followed by and compared to the interaction term with the green culture (Table 3.7).

Personal and Professional Traits. For the gold culture (i.e. gold*oa_pub as the dependent variable, Table 3.6), our regression results confirm the non-linear relationship between *seniority* and the likelihood to publish in OA journals. This is closely related to *professional status*; holding a PhD significantly increases a gold-culture researcher's likelihood to publish in OA journals. Interestingly and different from our more general findings for all groups, we now identify a positive and strongly significant effect of being employed at a *research institute*, as opposed to a university. That is, scholars from research institutes engaged in gold culture disciplines publish significantly more of their research in OA journals than their colleagues from universities in the same disciplines. Recall that our general regression in Table 3.5 showed a significant negative impact of the 'institute' variable. One possible explanation of this difference is that the pressure to publish in highly ranked journals may be greater in research institutes than in faculties. In this regard, we find that respondents at research institutes on average assess the importance of publications in refereed journals at 3.81 (as compared to 3.68 for university researchers), and the importance of the ranking of a journal at 3.51 (3.46 for university researchers) – a significant difference in both cases. Of course, this difference between university and institute researchers differs considerably between disciplines. However, our findings show that as the importance of journal publications in a specific field of research rises, institute researchers are disproportionately exposed to a 'publish or perish'-environment. Since highly reputed OA journals exist only in the gold culture, this specific publication pressure might explain the significant positive impact of the *institute* variable for scholars of that culture. This explanation is confirmed by the significantly higher impact of the *refereed journals* variable for the gold culture compared to the general impact as indicated in Table 3.6 (see below). However, the question remains why the *institute* variable also has a significant positive impact with scholars from the green culture (Table 3.7). Maybe in these disciplines research institutes tend to focus on areas where more OA journals are available.

Inherent Reward Structure. The reward structure in gold culture disciplines reveals that the *number of publications, refereed journals* and the *ranking* (i.e. the impact factor) of a journal all increase a researcher's likelihood to publish in OA journals, which stands in strong contrast to the general impact of these variables (Table 3.5). Conversely, the *number of monographs* has a significant negative impact. This holds for the gold culture as well as for the green culture (see also Table 3.7). For gold road researchers, it seems that publishing journal articles is important for their careers and that OA journals of high reputation are available. In the green culture, too, researchers strive for journal publications, but the established and highly esteemed journals are mostly closed-access. Last but not least, researchers of the gray culture seem to be less enthusiastic about either road – monographs are more important for their careers than journal articles (see Table A.3.3 in Appendix 3).

Personal opinion about OA. Not surprisingly, we again find that the researchers' personal opinions influence their use of the gold road of OA, especially in the gold culture. Interestingly and in contrast to researchers of the green culture, here we find that the perceived *quality* of OA journals and their *readership* advantage promote OA publications and that the coefficients are very similar to those in the general regression (Table 3.5).

Assessment of OA per Discipline and Region. Using the *awareness* and *relevance* factors as determinants of choosing the gold road yields an interesting insight, and also a difference to what we have observed so far. While both factors were also important drivers of OA publications in earlier regressions and while both still increase the explanatory power of the model, we now find that *relevance* is even more important than *awareness* for gold culture researchers (Table 3.6). In fact, the coefficient on relevance is more than twice that on awareness. This accords with our previous argument. Since most scholars in these disciplines are aware of OA journals, 'awareness' does not contribute much to explaining their choosing such journals. Researchers of the gold culture choose OA journals because these journals happen to be the ones with the highest impact factors and thus serve their careers. Moreover, we also find that this observation particularly applies to gold culture researchers from *emerging market economies*: Being from India, Egypt, Brazil or Russia increases the likelihood for scholars of the gold culture to publish in an OA journal by five to almost ten times compared to the average over all disciplines for scholars from the same region (as reported in Table 3.5). One possible explanation is the tradition of prominent OA publishers with a focus on medicine and related disciplines in these countries, such as Hindawi Publishing in Cairo and Medknow Publications in Mumbai (see chapter 2.3.1.1). According to the DOAJ, OA publishers in Brazil and, to a lesser extent, in Russia also tend to focus on disciplines that we classify as 'gold culture'.

We now compare the previous findings to the results of a binary logit regression that has an interaction term with the green culture (green*oa_pub) as its dependent variable (Table 3.7). Three important differences may be highlighted. First, the non-linear influence of *seniority* does not hold for the green culture. Instead, we find a significant but weak positive linear relationship: The longer a green culture academic spends in academia, the more likely she is to embrace OA journals. Second, the personal opinion of a green culture researcher regarding the *quality* of OA journals does not seem to affect the likelihood to publish in OA journals. Most interestingly, such respondents do not seem to share the view that OA journals have a strong *readership* advantage over CA journals. Third, while the *awareness* of OA publishing has a significant positive impact on the likelihood of gold road OA publishing, we see no impact for the *relevance* factor. This may be because, on the one hand, the green culture includes two disciplines with very low shares of publications in OA journals ('Mathematics and Statistics' and 'Business and Economics'). This is in line with our finding from chapter 2 that OA journals in *green disciplines* have lower impact factors (reputation) on average. Due to the inherent reward structure in these disciplines, we see less use of the gold road to OA. On the other hand, the green culture includes 'Physics and Astronomy', where more than half of the respondents have experience with both roads of OA.[18] Thus, the heterogeneity of the green culture in this respect may lead to an averaging out of the impact of the perceived relevance of gold OA.

3.3.3   The Green Road

Table 3.8 reports our binary logit estimates regarding the green road of OA. Specification (1) considers the respondents' personal and professional traits, as well as aspects of the inherent reward system. Specifications (2) to (4) successively add variables regarding the respondents' personal opinions about the *importance, readership* and *quality* of online repositories in their specific disciplines.

Personal and Professional Traits. In contrast to our observations regarding the gold road, we find that *seniority* does not affect the likelihood of using the green road. This result seems plausible since, first of all, access to a repository generally does not depend on academic experience to the same degree as access to a (refereed) OA journal. Secondly, even experienced scholars often like to upload first versions of their papers on repositories, be it to receive some feedback for a follow-up publication in a refereed journal or to bring new thoughts on current issues to public attention as quickly as possible. However, we still find that a researcher's *professional* status significantly increases her likelihood of using the green road. As long as professionals tend to have more publications, this result

---

[18]   Because of this dual nature of the discipline, in Appendix 3 we also discuss the results of a regression that excludes 'Physics and Astronomy' (see Table A.3.4).

Table 3.8   Basic regression models on the green road of OA

Variables	(1)	(2)	(3)	(4)
years_acad	−0.00269	0.0107	4.08e−06	−0.000492
	(0.00240)	(0.00852)	(0.00249)	(0.00260)
years_acad^2		−0.000240		
		(0.000184)		
professional	0.864***	0.832***	0.876***	0.952***
	(0.0838)	(0.0917)	(0.0850)	(0.0885)
institute		0.291***	0.290***	0.242***
		(0.0764)	(0.0764)	(0.0789)
no_publication	−0.0508	−0.0347	−0.0350	−0.0253
	(0.0365)	(0.0382)	(0.0381)	(0.0402)
no_monograph	0.0556**	0.0196	0.0200	−0.00677
	(0.0267)	(0.0279)	(0.0278)	(0.0292)
refereed_j	0.0445	0.0555	0.0560	0.0458
	(0.0507)	(0.0539)	(0.0539)	(0.0567)
j_ranking	0.116***	0.0888**	0.0893**	0.0908**
	(0.0387)	(0.0409)	(0.0409)	(0.0435)
rep_importance		0.239***	0.239***	0.0893***
		(0.0259)	(0.0258)	(0.0280)
rep_readership		0.354***	0.355***	0.230***
		(0.0302)	(0.0302)	(0.0318)
rep_citation		0.00888	0.00878	−0.0423
		(0.0283)	(0.0283)	(0.0301)
rep_quality				0.448***
				(0.0183)
Discipline dummies	YES	YES	YES	YES
Country dummies	YES	YES	YES	YES
Observations	10,468	10,468	10,468	10,468
Pseudo R²	0.134	0.190	0.190	0.244

Notes: Robust standard errors in parentheses. Constant not reported. *** p<0.01,
** p<0.05, * p<0.1.

seems reasonable – given the motives mentioned above for experienced scholars to use the green road. Moreover, and also in contrast to our findings for the basic regression results for gold OA (see Table 3.4), our estimates show that being with a *research institute* rather than a (public) university significantly increases the likelihood to use green OA outlets. This may be due to the fact that many research institutes run their own institutional repositories and expect their members to use them.

Inherent Reward System. Also in contrast to our findings for the gold road, the inherent reward system is not a major driver of green OA usage, with the sole exception of *journal ranking*, where we see a significant but relatively weak positive influence. Maybe the higher relevance of journal ranking induces scholars to upload preliminary versions of their work to collect feedback and to thus improve the chances of acceptance in a refereed journal. However, we must not overinterpret this relatively small coefficient.

Personal Opinions about OA. A total of three variables reflect the respondents' personal opinions about OA repositories. Including these variables clearly improves the explanatory power of our model. Not surprisingly, the perceived *importance* of publications in OA repositories has a significantly positive impact on the likelihood of using the green road. Most interestingly, green OA seems to be regarded as a means to increase the *readership*, but not the *citations*, of one's work. Indeed, readership has a strongly significant and positive impact on the use of online repositories. Moreover, the regression results indicate that the perception of *quality* in such (field-specific) forums is a good predictor as to why researchers provide free access to their papers via OA repositories. We will see later that both the perceived quality and the readership advantage are indeed dependent on the publishing cultures (see Tables 3.10 and 3.11).

Relying again on the categorization introduced in the context of Figure 3.11, we expand our analysis of the green road by differentiating between the three publishing cultures (gold, gray and green).[19] Table 3.9 shows the results of our binary logit estimates, incorporating gold and green culture dummies throughout specifications (2) to (5). Instead of separate country dummies, the estimations summarized in the table also use regional dummies, as defined above. We will again structure our analysis along the four groups of explanatory variables (personal and professional traits, inherent reward system, personal opinions about OA, and the average assessment of OA, using the culture and regional dummies).

Personal and Professional Traits. As with the findings reported in Table 3.8, we cannot identify a significant impact of *seniority*, with the exception of significant but weak coefficients in the non-linear specification (3).[20]

---

[19]   In Appendix 3 we also discuss the results of a regression that excludes 'Physics and Astronomy' (see Table A.3.5).

[20]   The maximum of the inverted u-shaped function of the likelihood to use repositories occurs at 20.5 years, i.e. at the age of 45.5 years if we assume that entry into academia takes place at the age of 25. This is more than seven years earlier than in the case of the gold road.

Table 3.9   Specific regression models on the green road of OA

Variables	(1)	(2)	(3)	(4)	(5)
years_acad	−0.00142	−0.00186	0.0163**	0.000816	0.000469
	(0.00231)	(0.00225)	(0.00805)	(0.00236)	(0.00248)
years_acad^2			−0.000397**		
			(0.000173)		
professional	0.955***	0.928***	0.851***	0.941***	1.015***
	(0.0815)	(0.0805)	(0.0874)	(0.0817)	(0.0850)
institute		0.217***	0.283***	0.269***	0.203***
		(0.0715)	(0.0691)	(0.0717)	(0.0744)
no_publication	−0.0871**	−0.0920***	−0.0939***	−0.0532	−0.0405
	(0.0345)	(0.0342)	(0.0343)	(0.0357)	(0.0373)
no_monograph	0.0275	0.0452*	0.0486**	0.0178	−0.0136
	(0.0255)	(0.0235)	(0.0236)	(0.0248)	(0.0261)
refereed_j	0.0203	0.0235	0.0178	0.00721	0.0287
	(0.0422)	(0.0417)	(0.0418)	(0.0441)	(0.0469)
j_ranking	0.0946***	0.0687**	0.0716**	0.0823**	0.0811**
	(0.0346)	(0.0338)	(0.0340)	(0.0359)	(0.0381)
rep_importance				0.225***	0.0745***
				(0.0245)	(0.0268)
rep_readership				0.365***	0.237***
				(0.0292)	(0.0312)
rep_citation				0.00716	−0.0403
				(0.0272)	(0.0294)
rep_quality					0.453***
					(0.0177)
west	−0.229*	−0.201	−0.234*	−0.105	−0.124
	(0.122)	(0.123)	(0.123)	(0.126)	(0.134)
east	−0.630***	−0.613***	−0.645***	−0.769***	−0.739***
	(0.143)	(0.143)	(0.144)	(0.147)	(0.154)
south	0.103	0.0611	0.0426	0.0604	−0.00665
	(0.126)	(0.126)	(0.127)	(0.130)	(0.137)
emerg	−0.401***	−0.437***	−0.458***	−0.479***	−0.524***
	(0.144)	(0.143)	(0.144)	(0.149)	(0.158)
green		1.107***	1.099***	0.978***	0.777***
		(0.0595)	(0.0596)	(0.0613)	(0.0642)
gold		−0.765***	−0.793***	−0.622***	−0.521***
		(0.0612)	(0.0619)	(0.0640)	(0.0664)
Discipline dummies	YES	NO	NO	NO	NO
Country dummies	NO	NO	NO	NO	NO
Observations	10,468	10,468	10,468	10,468	10,468
Pseudo R²	0.089	0.091	0.150	0.150	0.209

Notes: Robust standard errors in parentheses. Constant not reported. *** p<0.01, ** p<0.05, * p<0.1.

Again, both the *professional* and the *institute* dummy variables have a positive effect on green OA usage.

Inherent Reward System. Only the *journal ranking* variable has a strongly significant and slightly positive impact on green OA publishing (cf. the discussion of the results in Table 3.8).

Personal Opinions about OA. In this regard, our findings from Table 3.8 are confirmed. All three relevant aspects point in the same direction; they positively drive the decision towards green OA, and their inclusion improves the explanatory power of the model. Again, with the exception of *citation*, the perception of repository *readership* and *quality* in particular promote the use of such outlets. Yet the situation changes entirely once we look at the different publishing cultures. This takes us to an assessment of green OA per region and publishing culture.

Impact of Regions and Publishing Cultures. Looking at *regional effects*, we see, first of all, that essentially all regions have a significantly lower willingness to use green OA options than the reference region, the USA. The effect is strongest for Eastern Europe, followed by the emerging market economies. This differs considerably from what we found for the gold road, where the emerging market economies were particularly prone to using OA outlets. This result comes as no surprise in light of our choice of the US as the reference country. As we showed in chapter 2, Table 2.10, the USA hosts almost twice as many repositories as the country that ranks second (the UK), whereas Eastern European countries and emerging market economies in particular lag behind. Looking in turn at the effects of *publishing cultures*, we can identify a strongly significant effect that goes in two directions. While, as per our definition, members of the green culture are significantly more open to green OA (with coefficients ranging from around 0.8 to more than1.1), we find the very opposite for members of the gold OA culture, with coefficients ranging from around -0.5 to almost -0.8. This latter result is easily explained. Since the gold OA culture is dominated by Health Science and Biology, where journals typically refuse papers that have already been uploaded to a repository (the Ingelfinger rule), scholars tend to avoid the green road (see above, chapter 2.3.1.2). Ultimately, the results confirm our delineation of the publication cultures.

The impact of the publishing culture is not very surprising, as we found discipline-specific traits also for gold OA usage. Nevertheless, this picture calls for a more detailed look at both publishing cultures (gold versus green) in order to identify the specific impact of certain cultural traits. For this purpose, we ran additional regressions with an interaction between repository usage and cultural membership as the dependent variable. The results are reported in Tables 3.10 (gold*rep_pub) and 3.11 (green*rep_pub).

Table 3.10 *Green road regression results for the interaction with the gold OA culture*

Variables	(1)	(2)	(3)	(4)
years_acad	0.0113***	0.0115***	0.0581***	0.0113***
	(0.00416)	(0.00419)	(0.0181)	(0.00427)
years_acad^2			−0.00102***	
			(0.000382)	
professional	0.737***	0.733***	0.537***	0.645***
	(0.178)	(0.178)	(0.199)	(0.180)
institute		0.367***	0.376***	0.407***
		(0.122)	(0.122)	(0.124)
no_publication	0.132*	0.175**	0.177**	0.228***
	(0.0700)	(0.0720)	(0.0720)	(0.0747)
no_monograph	−0.219***	−0.245***	−0.245***	−0.258***
	(0.0415)	(0.0426)	(0.0428)	(0.0434)
refereed_j	0.231**	0.239**	0.236**	0.273**
	(0.107)	(0.107)	(0.107)	(0.108)
j_ranking	0.138*	0.142*	0.140*	0.118
	(0.0716)	(0.0728)	(0.0730)	(0.0755)
rep_importance		0.0950**	0.0961**	0.0620
		(0.0477)	(0.0478)	(0.0471)
rep_readership		0.00759	0.00534	0.0233
		(0.0515)	(0.0516)	(0.0514)
rep_citation		−0.0483	−0.0467	−0.0508
		(0.0511)	(0.0512)	(0.0511)
rep_quality		0.217***	0.217***	0.214***
		(0.0333)	(0.0334)	(0.0335)
institute		0.367***	0.376***	0.407***
		(0.122)	(0.122)	(0.124)
west				0.208
				(0.284)
east				−0.0388
				(0.329)
south				0.547*
				(0.287)
emerg				0.817***
				(0.300)
Observations	10,468	10,468	10,468	10,468
Pseudo R^2	0.023	0.042	0.044	0.049

Notes: Robust standard errors in parentheses. Constant not reported. *** p<0.01, ** p<0.05, * p<0.1.

The economics of open access

Table 3.11 *Green road regression results for the interaction with the green OA culture*

Variables	(1)	(2)	(3)	(4)
years_acad	−0.00445	−0.00208	−0.0115	−0.00109
	(0.00339)	(0.00367)	(0.0119)	(0.00376)
years_acad^2			0.000212	
			(0.000260)	
professional	0.822***	0.926***	0.963***	0.957***
	(0.121)	(0.128)	(0.132)	(0.128)
institute		0.335***	0.334***	0.324***
		(0.101)	(0.101)	(0.102)
no_publication	−0.183***	−0.0669	−0.0675	−0.0884*
	(0.0472)	(0.0524)	(0.0524)	(0.0533)
no_monograph	−0.311***	−0.478***	−0.478***	−0.454***
	(0.0330)	(0.0386)	(0.0386)	(0.0389)
refereed_j	0.225***	0.297***	0.297***	0.288***
	(0.0766)	(0.0880)	(0.0880)	(0.0855)
j_ranking	0.213***	0.238***	0.238***	0.229***
	(0.0513)	(0.0577)	(0.0578)	(0.0575)
rep_importance		0.119***	0.119***	0.138***
		(0.0373)	(0.0373)	(0.0388)
rep_readership		0.436***	0.437***	0.432***
		(0.0503)	(0.0503)	(0.0507)
rep_citation		−0.144***	−0.145***	−0.134***
		(0.0401)	(0.0402)	(0.0405)
rep_quality		0.646***	0.646***	0.639***
		(0.0325)	(0.0325)	(0.0324)
west				0.464**
				(0.221)
east				−0.143
				(0.255)
south				0.352
				(0.226)
emerg				0.179
				(0.252)
Observations	10,468	10,468	10,468	10,468
Pseudo R^2	0.031	0.224	0.224	0.227

Notes: Robust standard errors in parentheses. Constant not reported. *** p<0.01, ** p<0.05, * p<0.1.

Personal and Professional Traits. In contrast to our general findings in Tables 3.8 and 3.9, here we find a strongly significant non-linear relationship between *seniority* and green road usage for the gold culture disciplines (Table 3.10): Gold culture respondents deposit more of their works the longer they have been in academia, up to the threshold of about 28.5 years. However, the same does not hold for respondents from the green culture (Table 3.11). Interestingly, both tables exhibit a significant and strong positive impact of the variables *professional* and *institute* on green road usage.

Inherent Reward Structure. While the expectation of publications in *refereed journals* and the role of *journal ranking* have a significant and strong positive impact on the use of the green road for members of both cultures, the impact of the *number of publications* is significantly positive for members of the gold culture, but (in some specifications significantly) negative for members of the green culture.

Personal Opinion about OA. Again, the inclusion of the four opinion variables clearly improves the explanatory power of the model, in particular for members of the green culture (Table 3.11). Most interestingly, neither *readership* nor *citation* have a significant impact on the uploading of papers for scholars of the gold culture (Table 3.10), whereas there is a significant and strong positive impact of *readership* and a significantly negative impact of *citation* for scholars of the *green culture* (Table 3.11). It seems plausible that scholars from disciplines that feature many high-quality refereed OA journals generate readership in particular via publications in OA journals, rather than by uploading their papers to OA repositories. The negative impact of expected citations on green OA use is somewhat more difficult to interpret. Perhaps members of the green culture often use repositories to upload preliminary papers for discussion with the ultimate aim of publishing the final version in a CA journal. These authors strive for readership, but not citations, which are expected from the final CA publication.

Impact of Regions. Most interestingly, there is a significant and strong positive impact for gold-culture scholars from *emerging market economies* on the likelihood of using OA repositories (Table 3.10). This stands in clear contrast to the results regarding scholars from emerging market economies in general (Table 3.9), where we saw a significant negative impact. Thus, in emerging market economies, there seem to be strong forces that induce scholars from the 'gold OA disciplines' to publish in OA journals, as well as to upload papers on OA repositories.

3.4   GENERAL CONCLUSIONS

In this chapter, we have discussed the results of an international survey of scholarly authors' perceptions of and attitudes towards gold and green OA. The most important results from descriptive statistics and several regressions confirm and specify in more detail the findings of our analysis of some objective data on OA publishing in chapter 2.

Most importantly, the likelihood of publishing articles in OA journals (the gold road) or uploading papers to OA repositories (the green road) largely depends on the *discipline* the scholar is affiliated with. This impact is in turn driven by the discipline-specific reward systems and the varying availability of high-quality OA journals and repositories in the individual disciplines. By contrast, the scholars' *country* of residence generally makes little difference. Scholarly communication is typically an international affair, and the leading OA journals and repositories attract academic authors from across the world. Only in isolated instances did we observe country-specific patterns. This latter point might be due, firstly, to the fact a number of disciplines, typically in the humanities, often deal with country-specific issues that are communicated in the local language. Secondly, a number of specific support mechanisms exist for scholars from less developed countries to create the necessary infrastructure for free access to articles via international networks or to reduce publication fees for authors from such countries.[21]

In the following chapter, we will discuss some important policy implications that derive from our findings in chapters 2 and 3. In particular, we will show that any policy on OA publishing that does not take into account the specific incentive patterns in the individual disciplines is bound to fail.

---

[21]   These results also comply with the findings by Migheli and Ramello (2013) that the social norms governing scholarly publishing vary across disciplines and national boundaries.

4. Policy implications and the way forward

4.1 ALTERNATIVE POLICY INSTRUMENTS

As we know from the preceding chapters, the debate on OA publishing was triggered by two developments: First, rising journal prices placed pressure on academic library budgets. Second, as a consequence, smaller academic institutions and the broader public are inefficiently excluded from access to important research results. These problems seem to call for some form of policy intervention in the scholarly journal market (Armstrong 2015: F19).

Several policy instruments are available, and some of them have already been applied, with varying degrees of success. Antitrust law is generally less suitable because the market power of academic publishers mainly derives from their holding some highly specific and important journals, and to a lesser extent from some aggregate measure of market power in 'the market for academic journals'. Some academic libraries have established consortia in order to create some countervailing power when negotiating package deals with academic publishers. However, the libraries' bargaining power is limited by the fact that they cannot afford to discontinue subscriptions to important journals. The DEAL project provides a good example of the difficulties of German academic libraries to successfully bargain with the major academic publishers. This initiative was commissioned by the Alliance of Science Organisations in Germany to conclude nationwide licensing agreements with major academic publishers for the entire portfolio of electronic journals from 2017 onwards, including an open access component. The negotiations began with Elsevier and were scheduled to be continued with Springer Nature and Wiley. To improve their bargaining power, about 60 German academic institutions terminated their existing license agreements with Elsevier at the end of 2016. However, as of September 2017, no new license agreement with Elsevier has been reached.[1]

---

[1] See www.projekt-deal.de/about-deal and www.german-u15.de/presse/DEAL. html. For more details see Vogel and Kupferschmidt (2017).

Another policy outside of OA could be for universities or research sponsors to prevent their scholars from publishing in overpriced journals. However, this policy could conflict with the freedom of research. Moreover, some journals are expensive not because of the publisher's high profit margin but because of high unit production costs. The remaining instruments refer to a transition to OA, be it gradually (bottom up) or radically (top down), in combination with the abolishment of copyright protection for academic articles, or various hybrids of these measures. Whereas gold OA could, in the extreme case, completely replace the traditional system of journal publishing, green OA would typically complement publications in CA or OA journals.

4.2   THE FINANCIAL VIABILITY OF A LARGE-SCALE TRANSITION TO GOLD OA

In chapter 2, we showed that the number of OA journals and OA repositories has increased drastically since the turn of the millennium. However, a truthful depiction of the growing importance of OA in scholarly publishing would require information about the changing proportion of OA publications among all scholarly articles. An estimate of that proportion is not readily available for a number of reasons, including the treatment of hybrid journals, embargo periods, Robin Hood OA, multiple repositories and so on. If we consider only gold OA, specifically OA journals listed in the DOAJ, their share among all journals has increased from about 4 percent in 2009 to about 10 percent in September 2017.[2] A different picture emerges if we also include green OA: A study initiated by the European Commission estimated that of all scholarly papers published in the period 2007–12, more than 50 percent were available open access as of April 2014, a significantly higher share than in 1996 (below 30 percent), and that this proportion varies widely across disciplines (Archambault et al. 2014: vii; 24). Two other studies estimated proportions of only around 20 percent for 2008 and 2010, respectively (Gargouri et al. 2012; Björk et al. 2010).

Several calculations have shown that a large-scale transition from the subscription model to the gold road of open access, with article processing charges (APCs) being covered by the authors or their sponsors, is generally possible without additional money being required to fund academic journals, since the existing funds would just be reallocated from

---

[2]   See Shavell (2010: 333) and the update found at the websites of the DOAJ and 'Genamics Journal Seek'.

subscription fees to APCs. For example, Schimmer et al. (2015) present the following calculations: According to various market reports, annual global revenues from the sale of academic journals have amounted to approximately EUR 7.6 billion in recent years. This figure covers around two million articles, which yields a price per article of about EUR 3,800. If we restrict the analysis to articles listed on the Web of Science (around 1.5 million), the calculated revenues per article increase to approximately EUR 5,000. In 2014, the German Max Planck Society collected 1,046 APC invoices totalling EUR 1.3 million (including taxes), for an average APC of EUR 1,258. Similar figures apply to other institutions: Universities supported by the German Research Foundation reported an average APC of EUR 1,239;[3] the Austrian Science Fund arrives at EUR 1,282. The Wellcome Trust reports EUR 2,495 per article. This comparatively large amount is due to the Trust's funding of hybrid APCs, which differs from Germany and many other countries. Without hybrid journals, the average APC of the Wellcome Trust stands at EUR 1,686. Thus, average APCs are currently well below the EUR 2,000 cap imposed by the German Research Foundation[4] and far below the calculated revenues per article in the subscription model.

Journal prices are largely determined by the costs borne by the publishers, modified by their market power, which enables them to charge a mark-up on their cost (see chapter 2.2). In general, a publisher's article production cost will increase with rejection rates, the number of special graphics, article length, the share of non-article pages (such as cover, table of content, editorial, letters, book reviews and so on) and the rigour of the peer review, and they will decrease with circulation and the size of the publisher's portfolio. Moreover, the costs per article also depend on the mode of publication – print, online or both (King 2007: 94, 104; Houghton et al. 2009: 64).[5]

An interesting question in this context is to what extent alternative publishing models, such as the traditional subscription model or the gold

---

[3] A more recent study by Jahn and Tullney (2016: 7) reports average payments by German universities and research institutions of between EUR 1,239 and EUR 1,423 in the period 2011 to 2015.

[4] See the funding guidelines at www.dfg.de/formulare/12_20_en.pdf.

[5] The required publishing software accounts for a major component of the cost of establishing and running an electronic journal. The availability of standardized open-source software has drastically reduced publishers' costs of running electronic-only journals. In 2002, the Public Knowledge Project at the University of British Columbia launched the open-source journal management software Open Journal Systems, which has helped cut the publishing cost of many OA journals. For more details, see Willinsky (2009: xxiv and chapter 5).

and green road of OA, affect publishers' costs. Houghton et al. (2009) have studied the costs and potential benefits of alternative scholarly publishing models in the UK.[6] They estimate that in 2007, for electronic-only journals, the average cost per article to the publisher (excluding the costs of external peer review and VAT) amounted to GBP 2,337 for the subscription model and GBP 1,524 for gold OA publication. This implies that the transition from toll access to gold OA would reduce average publication costs per article by 35 percent (for dual-mode journals, this figure stands at 38 percent). The transition from the subscription model to green OA with full service overlay, including managing the peer review process, editing, proofing and hosting, with commercial margins, would even reduce publishers' cost per article by 46 percent (ibid: 159).

By contrast, in addition to the publishers' expenses, the *social* cost of journal publishing would also include the costs borne by authors, reviewers, libraries and final users. Houghton et al. (2009: 183–84) estimate the total cost of writing,[7] peer reviewing, publishing and dissemination per article in electronic-only journals at GBP 8,296 for the subscription model, GBP 7,483 for gold OA and GBP 7,115 for green OA. The cost differences between the modes of publication are mostly due to the costs associated with rights management and copyright protection activities, including in particular the costs of access control and authentication systems (borne by publishers and readers), the costs of handling permissions by using standard and/or more open licensing and blanket permissions (borne by publishers and users), the costs of licensing negotiations (borne by publishers and libraries), and the costs of copyright agreements with authors (borne by publishers and authors), all of which will be much reduced or altogether avoided by a transition to OA.[8]

We can conclude that a large-scale transition from the subscription model to the gold road of open access would be financially viable for the academic community and would even reduce the total funds required of

---

[6]   Intensive discussions ensued regarding the implications of the study by Houghton et al. (2009) and the reliability of the underlying cost figures. See, for example, the response by Harnad et al. (2010).

[7]   The average time to write a journal article is estimated at 95 hours (Houghton et al. 2009: 146), and the cost of writing the article is estimated at GBP 5,328 (ibid.: 184). This implies an hourly rate of around GBP 56.

[8]   The radical proposal by Shavell to eliminate copyright for scholarly articles would lead to the most drastic reduction of these transaction costs: '. . .the elimination of copyright would mean that publishers would not invest resources in charging readers, making copyright arrangements with authors, granting licenses to others, or in protecting their copyrights through search for violations and through litigation' (Shavell 2010: 330).

universities, research institutes and research sponsors to finance academic journal publishing – provided the average APC would not increase drastically as a consequence of the transition. In particular, the transition would come at no extra cost to universities, even if they refrain from passing on the APCs to the authors. Shavell (2010: 321 f.) argues that universities will have an incentive to financially reward their researchers' publication efforts in order to maintain or increase their reputation and to attract more faculty, students, gifts and grants. Any such incentive will be especially pronounced for universities that rely on tuition fees and endowments, like private universities in the US, as opposed to mainly publicly-funded universities, like most universities in Continental Europe. Regardless of this, the figures show that a general shift from the subscription model to the open access model would be financially viable in a static environment with fixed university budgets, a given number of journals and fixed publication fees per article. In a dynamic environment, however, these general calculations must be qualified in several respects.

First, as university budgets are cut, there will be pressure on the faculties/departments to save on subscription fees by dropping some journals or to reduce publication fee subsidies, e.g. by raising the requirements for eligibility. We expect that publication fee subsidies are more easily reduced than subscription fees: Discontinuing the subscription to a specific journal will stir opposition from all potential readers and all regular contributors to this journal who are employed by the university. Conversely, if a university refuses to subsidize an author's publication fees, only this author will protest. Of course, a coalition of authors might emerge, even though one has to take into account that their interests are not homogeneous. Moreover, the readers will have no direct voice anymore.

Secondly, publishers of leading journals have strong bargaining power and will be tempted to exploit authors by raising their APCs to maintain their rate of return. However, the ability and willingness of universities to cover these costs has its limits. This problem can be countered by several strategies, such as granting budgets to individual faculty members to induce them to search for lower fees, monitoring fees for reasonableness (Shavell 2010: 322), or capping publication fee subsidies. Note also that overly generous subsidization of publication fees could lead to a socially excessive level of publications (Shavell 2010: 326).

Thirdly, even if the large-scale transition from the subscription model to the OA model is financially viable in aggregate terms, this need not apply on the micro-level. Any transition will produce winners and losers. The winners are those players who read much but publish little, whereas the losers are those who publish extensively, to the benefit of many readers. This need not be a problem between more versus less research-oriented universities, since the former will typically both publish more and subscribe to more journals, and vice versa. However, the situation is different between (research-oriented) universities versus practitioners, who tend to read but not to contribute to scholarly journals, such as lawyers, judges, physicians, the pharmaceutical industry, high-tech manufacturers and so on. In general, the top research universities would shoulder most of the burden with respect to author fees.[9]

Consequently, regardless of its financial viability on the aggregate level, the transition from the subscription model to gold OA will require some collective action to cope with a number of obstacles, including the unequal distribution of costs and benefits, first mover problems, and the strong bargaining power of the leading commercial publishers. Whether the existing efforts at collective action, some of which we have discussed in chapter 2, will prevail against these obstacles remains to be seen.

4.3 LIMITS TO OA

In light of the challenges of a transition to OA, it is no surprise that opposition to OA is forthcoming not only from academic publishers and their associations but also from many academic authors who object to the 'strange idea' of requiring them to pay to deliver their valuable output, who are not convinced of the quality of OA publications, or who are concerned about OA mandates potentially limiting their freedom of academic research. Let us discuss some potential problems of OA in more detail.

4.3.1 Limits to Gold OA

Regarding *gold OA*, many academic authors do not trust the *quality* of OA journals. They strongly prefer the established traditional journals 'with well understood quality assurance processes (particularly peer review) and trusted quality flags (especially journal titles as "brands")' (Pinfield 2015: 613), where quality is typically judged by a journal's impact factor. As long as both authors and readers rely on impact factors when deciding where to publish and what to read and cite, it remains difficult for OA journals to establish a strong reputation, given that they are typically much younger than traditional journals. Apart from this 'start-up problem', which would decline over time, the crucial question arises whether the OA business model creates systematic incentives to accept lower quality papers. At

---

[9] This point is stressed by Mueller-Langer and Watt (2010).

least those OA journals that depend mostly on APCs for revenue might be induced to accept more and more papers, at the expense of rigorous evaluation (McCabe and Snyder 2005; Agrawal 2014: 133).[10] Moreover, a direct transfer of money from authors to publishers might be a source of 'corruption': 'By adding a financial component to the front end of the scholarly publishing process, the open-access movement will ultimately corrupt scholarly publishing and hurt the communication and sharing of novel knowledge' (Beall 2013: 590).

'Corruption of scholarly publishing' refers not only to the publishers' incentives to neglect rigorous peer review in favor of larger revenues from publication fees. A 'new business model', which aims at exploiting inexperienced scholars or their sponsors by charging publication fees without providing adequate services, constitutes an extreme form of corruption. According to Jeffrey Beall, a librarian at the University of Colorado in Denver, some publishers of OA journals engage in 'predatory publishing', accepting articles with little or no peer review, listing academics as members of editorial boards without their permission, appointing fake academics to editorial boards, mimicking the name or website style of more established journals, and so on. In 2010, Beall established a list of predatory publishers (*'Beall's List'*), which was updated regularly until December 2016. This list sparked controversy from the very beginning and was attacked by the publishers concerned, as well as by open-access advocates, who argued Beall was motivated by a general ideological objection to OA that led him to exaggerate the problems (Pinfield 2015: 619; Anderson 2015). While Beall's List went offline in January 2017, its publication induced the DOAJ to tighten its inclusion criteria and to drop a number of suspicious journals.[11]

Closely related to the financing of OA journals is the question whether a transition from the subscription model to the OA model would create various types of *discrimination*, e.g. against authors from poor countries or universities, or against new and unpopular ideas. For low- and middle-income countries, many OA journals offer APC discounts of up to 100 percent. Sometimes discounts are also available to authors from richer countries who lack sufficient funds (Lawson 2015). And while the costs imposed on OA contributors from developing countries are often waived, any such authors are also consumers of literature, either directly or as

---

[10]   See also Armstrong (2015: F21). However, this incentive vanishes if the degradation of quality reduces the fee the journal can charge so far that profits suffer. See Shavell (2010: 334, fn. 74).

[11]   For more details, see the Wikipedia entry on 'predatory open access publishing', assessed 9 February 2017 at https://en.wikipedia.org/wiki/Predatory_open_access_publishing. See also Xia et al. (2015), as well as Wallace and Perri (2016).

BOX 4.1   RESEARCH4LIFE AND OA FOR DEVELOPING COUNTRIES

'Research4Life' is a program that addresses the importance and opportunities of OA to research results for developing countries. It includes four initiatives launched and supported by the World Health Organization: (1) Health Internetwork Access to Research Initiative (HINARI, founded in 2002); (2) Access to Global Online Research in Agriculture (AGORA, 2004); (3) Online Access to Research in the Environment (OARE, 2006); and (4) Access to Research for Development and Innovation (ARDI, 2009). Each of them seeks to provide researchers from eligible (research) institutions with free (band one countries) or reduced-fee (band two countries) access to research in the respective fields.[A] Once an institution has registered with one of the initiatives, all of its researchers receive access to the full content of the journals covered by the initiative. Each initiative cooperates with different (mostly closed access) publishers who offer free or reduced-fee access to their full portfolio of journals.

Mueller-Langer et al. (2016) analyze the treatment effect of the OARE initiative on research output by comparing member versus non-member institutions. Three results are of particular interest: First and foremost, the free or reduced-fee access to research in environmental science afforded by OARE raises the research output of member institutions by at least 43 percent. Second, this effect is stronger the more closely an institution is located to the country's largest city and the more highly its research is ranked. Third, OARE membership also matters as an input variable, meaning that researchers from member institutions make significantly more use of (freely) accessible OARE journal content.

Note: [A] Eligibility is subject to a total of five factors: (1) Total GNI, (2) GNI per capita, (3) the United Nations Least Developed Countries list, (4) the Human Development Index and (5) Health Life Expectancy. For more information see http://research4life.org.

---

library users, and open access will allow them to draw upon resources that would be unavailable under the subscription-based model (Suber and Arunachalam 2005; see also Box 4.1).

Thus, there are instruments to cope with the problems of a transition to OA in poor countries. However, there is a more general problem of a broad scale transition to OA on the international level. If significant 'international trade imbalances' exist in the sense that some countries are net exporters of OA research and others are net importers, and if, additionally, both the users (through libraries) and the producers (through refunds of APCs) are supported by national public funds, a switch from the subscription model to OA leads to a subsidization of taxpayers in 'reader countries' by taxpayers in 'author countries'.[12]

---

[12]   For a similar argument see Armstrong (2015: F21).

Another problem is how to cope with authors from relatively poor universities within a country. In this respect, the effects of a transition to OA crucially depend on who is to bear the publication fees. There are two extreme cases. On the one hand, each university could reallocate all expenditure on subscription fees, i.e. a fixed amount of money, to cover their authors' APCs. This would maximize the risk that high-quality papers by authors from poor universities will not be funded and therefore perhaps not be published. On the other hand, if any article accepted by any OA journal were to be financed from public funds, the risk of excessive publication arises: From a social welfare perspective, too much money is spent on the publication of low-quality papers.[13] An efficient system should publicly fund all accepted papers that meet a predetermined quality threshold. The greater the share of the benefits of publication that accrues to readers and users outside of universities, such as lawyers, judges, medical doctors, engineers and so on, as well as ultimately to the general public, the more public subsidies for publication fees are justified. The crucial task is to establish an efficient system of quality control.

Apart from the problem of discrimination against poor countries and poor universities, Beall (2013: 590) raises the alleged problem of discrimination against new and unpopular ideas: 'Popular ideas will receive funding; new and unpopular ideas, regardless of their merit, will remain unfunded.' However, this problem is not solely attributable to OA publishing; to some extent, it is characteristic of all forms of academic publishing. Mainstream articles are generally more likely to pass the review process than original and creative but heterodox ones. A prominent example is George Akerlof's 'The Market for Lemons', which was rejected by the *American Economic Review* and the *Review of Economic Studies* for 'triviality', and by the *Journal of Political Economy* for 'incorrectness'. Only on the fourth attempt, in 1970, was the paper published in the *Quarterly Journal of Economics*. In 2001, the article earned Akerlof the Nobel Memorial Prize in Economic Sciences, and it remains one of the most widely cited papers in modern economic theory.[14] Examples abound of leading journals rejecting, often repeatedly, now classic papers by leading economists, including Paul Samuelson, James Tobin, Gary Becker, Paul Krugman, Kenneth Arrow, Robert Lucas, Brian Arthur, Bertil Ohlin, Milton Friedman and many others (Gans and Shephard

---

[13] There is a similar problem with patent protection, where incentives to engage in R&D may be too weak or too strong (in which case a patent race may ensue). See Eger et al. (1992: 93–97).

[14] https://en.wikipedia.org/wiki/The_Market_for_Lemons.

1994). The crucial question is whether OA aggravates this problem. This again depends on the financing of the publication fees. If the fees were to be paid exclusively by the universities, there is a high probability of some new and creative papers that are not in line with the topics and approaches preferred by the university administration not being supported. However, the more competing funds with different policies are available and the more these funds rely on the journals' quality control, the lower the risk of OA systematically distorting the selection process.

Finally, a critical point concerns *mandates* by universities or research sponsors for the researchers they employ or support to publish their work in OA journals or repositories. Regarding OA journals, a mandate is clearly not helpful while many outlets still lack reputation, as remains the case in several disciplines, particularly in economics. More generally, mandates may conflict with the freedom of academic research. Beall (2013: 594) formulated this problem quite bluntly:

> A social movement that needs mandates to work is doomed to fail. A social movement that uses mandates is abusive and tantamount to academic slavery. Researchers need more freedom in their decisions not less. How can we expect and demand academic freedom from our universities when we impose oppressive mandates upon ourselves?

In Germany, Roland Reuß, professor of literary studies at the University of Heidelberg and a well-known opponent of OA publishing, criticized in no less drastic terms the proposal by the Federal Ministry of Education and Research to make OA publication mandatory for all research funded by the ministry, calling it 'state authoritarianism of Wilhelminian flavor'.[15] There is an ongoing discussion as to whether OA mandates would be compatible with Article 5(3) of the German Basic Law.[16] There appears to be a broad consensus among constitutional lawyers that this Article stipulates the freedom of researchers to decide *whether*, *where* and *when* to publish their results (Schmidt 2016; Link 2013). Recently, 17 professors of the University of Konstanz challenged before the competent administrative court a new statute regulating their obligation to exercise their secondary publication right,[17] which they consider incompatible with the above Article (*Forschung&Lehre*, No. 1/2017: 7).

---

[15] *Frankfurter Allgemeine Zeitung*, 28 September 2016: N4.
[16] 'Arts and sciences, research and teaching shall be free. The freedom of teaching shall not release any person from allegiance to the constitution.'
[17] See above, chapter 2.3.2.2.

4.3.2 Limits to Green OA

Regarding *green OA* more generally, the degree of substitutability may create problems. On one hand, if in addition to the version of an article published in a toll access journal, various pre- and post-print versions circulate on the internet, readers may have to incur additional search costs to ascertain which one is the definite or most suitable version. On the other hand, the more easily electronic versions of the paper are accessible online and the greater the degree of substitutability between them and the CA version, the lower are readers' search costs, but the greater is the threat to the business model of the publishers of traditional journals. This is why publishers often impose embargo periods or restrict green OA in other ways, for example by prohibiting uploads of the final format and excluding popular repositories. In some disciplines, such as medicine and biology, journals do not accept articles that have been uploaded to a repository prior to publication. Consequently, there are at least two limits to green OA mandates: First, if only a few countries or institutions adopt this policy, journals may be reluctant to accept papers from authors who are subject to these restrictions. Second, if a substantial number of countries were to coordinate their policies in this respect, some CA journals may be closed down due to inadequate profits from subscription fees.

A simple replacement of traditional journals by OA repositories obviously cannot solve these problems. Without journals, the repositories would have to take some of the journals' important functions, such as reviewing, selecting and formatting the papers. Otherwise the market for scholarly papers would be characterized by an inefficient over-production of non-reviewed and non-branded papers that serve neither to increase the authors' reputation nor to provide ex-ante orientation to readers as to the quality of the available papers.

4.4 FUNDAMENTAL REQUIREMENTS FOR AN EFFICIENT TRANSITION TO OA

When discussing the transition from the subscription model to gold OA, i.e. from a 'readers pay' to an 'authors/sponsors pay' model, one has to consider that not all types of academic output are suited for the (gold) OA business model. Articles in scholarly journals are excellent candidates for this transition because in most disciplines the authors publish not for money but for reputation. By contrast, the situation is completely different with respect to textbooks. In most disciplines, textbooks have little impact on the reputation of the author, who may, however, earn considerable royalties from book sales. The incentives to write a textbook would be destroyed if readers no longer paid a reasonable price (see also Armstrong 2015: F1, fn. 2).[18] With a view to what types of content are suited for OA, Shavell (2010: 337–39) offers a more fine-grained definition of 'academic work'. He employs four criteria to determine whether a journal – or, more generally, a work – is academic in nature: (1) the authors and/or the publisher are usually academics; (2) the readers are mainly academics; (3) the content is academic in character; (4) only low royalties are paid, if any. If a work qualifies as 'academic' and is thus principally suited for OA, the crucial question is how to limit the social costs associated with OA, which potentially include:

1) reduced incentives for academic publishers to publish scholarly articles;
2) weaker signal of paper quality, resulting in increased search costs for readers;
3) increased difficulties for universities to assess the quality of their academic staff;
4) censorship and restrictions on academic freedom.

We will discuss each of these concerns in turn.

4.4.1 Proper Incentives for Academic Publishers

With respect to OA journals (gold OA), the publication fees paid by the authors or sponsors must suffice for the publishers to cover their costs and to earn a reasonable profit. This implies that general caps on publication fees might discriminate against journals with high production cost. To avoid that kind of bias, sponsors should accept higher publication fees for high-cost journals.[19] Regarding OA repositories ('green OA'), the free availability of close substitutes to subscription-based journals must be

---

[18] Thus, it comes as no surprise that German academic publishers heavily criticize the intended amendments to German copyright law that would allow students and scholars to upload up to 25 percent of texts under copyright, including textbooks, as reading material. See, for example, the publisher Georg Siebeck's (2016) criticism of the report by Haucap et al. (2016) on the economic effects of such restrictions on copyright protection.

[19] Even though it is difficult for outsiders to determine the exact cost of a journal, proxies are available that facilitate the distinction between higher and lower cost journals. To avoid inefficiencies, not the actual costs but the minimum costs are decisive.

prevented from undermining the business model of journal publishers and thereby their incentive to publish.

There are essentially two ways to avoid this disincentive. First, the effect on traditional publishers' profits will be smaller the lower the degree of substitutability of the freely accessible repository version and the journal version of the article. In the case of perfect substitutes, i.e. identical versions, no-one will subscribe to the journal. Private publishers would refuse to publish those journals, and thus also to provide valuable services such as selecting, proofreading, formatting and distributing the articles. To prevent this, the uploaded articles must be sufficiently distinct from the journal versions, which is indeed what many publishers require (see chapter 2). However, as discussed above, this solution might yield a multitude of different available versions of an article, potentially confusing the readers. Second, publishers can be protected by embargo periods, i.e. by a sufficiently long delay between the publication of the journal article and its uploading to a free repository. For example, when the legislator grants scholarly authors an inalienable right to secondary publication (as has been the case in Germany since January 2014), the fact that the half-life of the articles differs dramatically among the disciplines must be taken into account (see chapter 2). Consequently, the embargo period should be longer for disciplines with longer average article half-lives (e.g. for humanities, as opposed to science).

4.4.2   Quality Assurance

Quality assurance is an important function of traditional, subscription-based journals. At least in disciplines that rely heavily on scholarly articles published in journals with a clear, widely-recognized quality ranking, such as in sciences, social sciences and economics, authors aim to publish their articles in the best journals, which is also where readers first look for literature. Journal rankings are based on citation scores and provide a valuable signal of quality to both authors and readers. Though far from perfect, this system provides incentives for journal publishers to improve the quality of the articles so that they may raise the subscription fees, and for academic authors to send their best articles to the best journals so that they enjoy the best reputation possible. This incentive may be less pronounced in OA journals that are financed by publication fees. As argued above, on the one hand, publishers of OA journals might be induced to increase the quantity and reduce the average quality of the accepted articles, as long as profits rise, the extreme form of this being predatory publishing. While every additional article in an OA journal financed via APCs means additional revenues for the publisher, albeit with some risk of future APCs declining, additional articles in a subscription-based journal may justify an increase of subscription fees in the future, provided that the subscribers value the additional benefit of more articles than the perceived loss in average quality. On the other hand, to the extent it becomes more expensive for an author to publish a paper in a highly ranked, discriminating journal, some authors might tend to submit their best papers to less prestigious journals, which would render the quality signals provided by different journals less precise (Armstrong 2015: F21–F22). Consequently, many authors have less faith in the quality of OA journals compared to traditional subscription-based journals. As we know from our survey (see chapter 3), an important reason for the large share of gold-road OA articles in biology, health and agriculture is the strong reputation of OA journals in these disciplines, with the reverse applying in particular to economics. Whatever the reasons for the early success of OA journals in some disciplines may be (see Box 4.2 below for a best-practice example), it should have become clear that the threat of predatory publishers makes the establishment and success of OA journals in other disciplines more difficult today than it was 20 years ago.

To establish a good reputation of OA journals in the lagging disciplines would require some collective action. One such strategy would be for OA-oriented research sponsors to pursue: They could support the leading scholars in a discipline in serving as members of the editorial board of a newly established OA journal, conducting rigorous quality monitoring and attracting excellent submissions (see the example of *PLOS Biology*). While journal reputation would take some time to grow, as soon as potential authors and readers are convinced that the journal guarantees high quality, publication in OA journals will begin to gain importance in such disciplines. Shavell has suggested another, more radical strategy. Assuming a systematic divergence between the interest of individual academics and the collective interest of all academics, he proposes to altogether abolish copyright protection for academic articles in a narrow sense (Shavell 2010: 335 f.):

> If an individual academic insists on open access to his or her publication, this single action brings about no real change in the overall system of copyrighted works – that system continues to exist. And because the system of copyright continues to exist, the academic who obtains open access for his or her work does not as a consequence obtain the benefits that would flow from the general abolition of academic copyright. That is, the academic does not enjoy free access to all academic works. Likewise, even if a university requires that there be open access to works published by its faculty members, the university will not then garner the benefits of free access to all academic works – the university will still have to pay for journals and for books. Hence, it may well be that a collective action, namely, one that ends the legal right to copyright academic works, is needed to achieve open access, or at least to achieve that objective soon.

BOX 4.2 PLOS BIOLOGY AS A BEST-PRACTICE EXAMPLE

In March 2001, Harold Varmus, Nobel Laureate and former Director of the National Cancer Institute, Patrick O. Brown, Professor at the Stanford University School of Medicine, and Michael Eisen, Assistant Professor at the University of California, Berkeley, founded the Public Library of Science (PLOS) as a non-for-profit publisher. In September that year, they circulated an open letter requiring science journals to provide open access to their full content:

> To encourage the publishers of our journals to support this endeavour, we pledge that, beginning in September 2001, we will publish in, edit or review for, and personally subscribe to only those scholarly and scientific journals that have agreed to grant unrestricted free distribution rights to any and all original research reports that they have published, through PubMed Central and similar online public resources, within 6 months of their initial publication date.[A]

Even though more than 30,000 signatories supported the call, neither did the publishers make any concessions nor was any significant action forthcoming from the signatories (Eckdahl 2004). Therefore, PLOS launched the first of its own journals, *PLOS Biology*, in October 2003, which only two years later already achieved an impact factor of 13.9, the highest in general biology (Suber 2006, 151), and has continued to score excellent impact factors ever since.[B]

Several factors have contributed to the extraordinary success of this OA journal (Eckdahl 2004):

- The journal was launched by outstanding experts in the field and has thus attracted many excellent scholars as authors and reviewers. It conducts rigorous quality controls and can afford to be very selective.
- This level of excellence in an area of great public interest (biology with applications in medicine) has helped the PLOS attract grants. Already in December 2002, a grant of USD 9 million was received from the Gordon and Betty Moore Foundation to establish an editorial board and staff.
- *PLOS Biology* is a full-service journal. Apart from research articles for an academic audience, it includes a number of sections that present the results of high-profile original research of great significance also to a variety of non-academic audiences, such as physicians, patients and policy makers. Even though these additional services do not necessarily affect citations (the impact factor), they boost readership and thereby social impact in a broader sense.

To ensure timely publication, reviewers are required to complete their evaluations within ten days. Of course, this is difficult to enforce. Actually, the median duration of the review process of *PLOS Biology* has increased from 100 days in 2003 to around 170 in 2015, whereas the duration of the production process has fallen slightly from around 60 days to less than 50 (Hartgerink 2017). This suggests that the publication delay is not much different from other journals in biology and similar disciplines (Powell 2016). The publication fee for papers accepted by *PLOS Biology* is USD 2,900 (originally USD 1,500).

Subsequently, PLOS has launched a number of additional journals, including *PLOS Medicine* in 2004 (also a highly selective journal, charging a publication fee of USD 2,900), *PLOS Computational Biology* in 2005 (USD 2,250), *PLOS Genetics* in 2005 (USD 2,250), *PLOS Pathogens* in 2005 (USD 2,250), *PLOS ONE* in 2006 (a mega-journal with multi-disciplinary orientation; acceptance is based on methodological rigor rather than novelty; acceptance rate of 70–80 percent; USD 1,495 publication fee),[C] *PLOS Neglected Tropical Diseases* in 2007 (supported by a USD 1.1 million grant from the Bill and Melinda Gates Foundation, publication fee of USD 2,250), and *PLOS Currents* in 2009 (a publication channel with a streamlined peer review process and no publication fee).

In 2010, PLOS became financially self-sufficient, covering its costs exclusively from publication fees. *PLOS ONE*, the mega-journal that has been publishing more than 20,000 articles a year since 2012, subsidizes smaller and more selective journals in the PLOS family. The PLOS Publication Fee Assistance Program supports authors who are unable to pay all or part of their publication fees (USD 3 million in 2014).[D] Since 2009, the Article-Level Metrics have provided a timely measure of article reach and impact, even before the accumulation of citations. PLOS recently stopped publishing traditional impact factors for its journals.

Notes: [A] www.plos.org/open-letter.
[B] www.bioxbio.com/if/html/PLOS-BIOL.html.
[C] For more details see also Armstrong (2015: F5): 'Publishing in a mega-journal is a strategy intermediate between publishing in a traditional selective journal and just posting a working paper on the Internet.'
[D] https://www.plos.org/faq#loc-plos-publication-fee-assistance.

With this strategy, subscription-based journals would no longer be viable and only OA journals would remain.

4.4.3   Proper Assessment of Scholars

The third potential problem is closely related to the second one. A greater difficulty of assessing the quality of articles before reading them translates directly to an increased difficulty of assessing applicants for academic positions – at least in those disciplines that strongly rely on articles published in highly ranked journals. What is the likely impact of OA on the assessment of scholars? This question is easily raised but difficult to answer. As mentioned above, insofar as quality control is less rigorous in OA journals, the costs of distinguishing between high-quality and low-quality articles, and thereby also the cost of assessing the quality of their authors, increase. In other words, the better the ex-ante quality control by

OA journals, the less additional problems a transition to OA journals will create for the assessment of scholars. And yet the transition to OA might also facilitate the assessment of scholars: If OA led to more citations, the basis of assessment would become more reliable. However, there seems to be no clear evidence of a citation bonus for OA articles, even though they are downloaded more frequently than toll access articles (Armstrong 2015: F7; McCabe and Snyder 2015). This may well change as the reputation of OA journals improves in all disciplines. In this case, the OA principle could facilitate the transition to a fairer assessment of scholarly authors in that the journal impact factor, which allows less frequently cited authors to free-ride on the success of some top stars in the same journal, could be replaced with the personal impact factor, which relies on the citation rates of specific articles.[20]

However, the assessment of the 'quality' of scholars or even entire universities based on journal impact factors or personal impact factors creates a more general problem: Such assessment induces scholars and universities to adapt their performance and the allocation of resources to these output-oriented measures, whose suitability is moreover doubtful. For example, scholars tend to engage in 'slicing': They 'divide their research into as many articles as possible in order to enlarge their publication list' (Osterloh and Frey 2014a: 9), or they 'distort their results to please, or at least not to oppose, possible reviewers' (ibid.). In general, 'output-related incentives tend to crowd out intrinsically motivated curiosity' (ibid.: 10), a motivation which has often led to pathbreaking scientific discoveries and technological innovations (see already the examples provided by Abraham Flexner (1939/2017), the founding director of the Institute of Advanced Studies at Princeton). Some universities have been known to pay highly cited researchers to agree to a second affiliation in their publications so that the universities' ranking will improve.[21] Since the end of the 1990s, a growing body of research has addressed the problems associated with journal rankings and impact factors (see for example Seglen 1997, Osterloh and Frey 2014a, b and Frey and Osterloh 2015 with many references). Bruno Frey and Margit Osterloh have suggested

---

[20] Randy Schekman (2013) of UC Berkeley, the 2013 Nobel laureate in Biology, pleads for a radical solution: All articles that meet the journal's editorial criteria should be published and made freely available to the public, financed by APCs or other revenues. 'Mega journals' such as *PLOS ONE* already follow this strategy to some extent (Armstrong 2015: F4–F5).

[21] Bhattacharjee (2011) reports that this strategy has allowed King Saud University in Riyadh to climb several hundred places in international rankings within four years.

replacing the prevailing system based on output and process control with an alternative system based on input control: a careful socialization and rigorous selection of faculty members, who are subsequently supplied with sufficient basic funds and enjoy a high degree of autonomy. This system may be supported by an open post-publication evaluation, which would make the assessment of a scholar's research output more expensive but also more reliable compared to the prevailing one-dimensional system based on journal impact factors. The spread of OA, which creates a broader base of readers, in conjunction with an open post-publication evaluation of scholarly articles could thus improve the incentives of scholars, departments and universities to allocate their resources to the socially most valuable research questions, which naturally comes at a price: higher search costs for readers.

4.4.4 Guarantee of Academic Freedom

Finally, it has been argued that OA might lead to censorship and other restrictions of academic freedom. There are two basic concerns. First, when subscription fees are replaced by publication fees, it is the universities, departments and research sponsors, rather than the readers, who decide which journals (articles) are funded. Second, if OA is enforced by mandates, scholars are no longer free to decide whether, when and where to publish their research results. Let us discuss these two points in some more detail.

Regarding the first concern, there are two extreme scenarios. The first one is a radical transition from the subscription model to the OA model envisaged by Shavell (2010). Due to the abolition of copyright on academic articles, all subscription journals would be replaced by OA journals and exclusively financed by the universities/departments. Then any researcher wishing to publish a paper in a scholarly (OA) journal would depend on a subsidy from her institution or would have to bear the publication fee herself. Such a system favours those authors whose papers are in line with the research goals of their institution, whereas previously a large number of independent journals decided which papers to publish. Thus, in this transition scenario, the decision about funding and, by implication, publishing an article is concentrated in fewer hands, which increases the risk of censorship. In the second scenario, the money saved from the abolition of the subscription model is allocated to a wide range of independent research sponsors, who reallocate their budget from subsidizing subscription fees to subsidizing publication fees and thus decide whose publication fees to cover. With a sufficiently large number of sponsors, the risk of censorship should be no greater than it is today.

In both scenarios, a wholesale transition to OA creates another problem, which concerns the authors' access to publication venues: Authors will find it more difficult to publish in OA journals than is the case today with traditional toll access journals. Whereas in the subscription model, acceptance for publication depends only on decisions by the referees and the editor, publication in OA journals requires an additional decision regarding the covering of the publication fees. Since more than one independent decision is required for access to a scarce resource (publication in a scholarly journal), the problem of the 'tragedy of the anticommons' (Heller 1998; Heller 2009) arises, which leads to that resource being underused, i.e. too few publications.

Let us now address the second point, OA *mandates*. Initially the question arises why mandates are even needed if we assume that scholars typically aim to maximize their readership. However, scholars hesitate to publish in *OA journals* while they perceive them as being of inferior quality, meaning that to publish in these journals could hurt their reputation. It would be pointless, and indeed illegal in many countries, to enforce the publication of research results against the authors' will,[22] or to prescribe the OA route of publication. As suggested above, it makes much more sense to support excellent scholars in establishing new, high-quality OA journals. Any success along these lines will reduce the need for OA mandates. Regarding *green OA*, we see no general problems associated with institutions obliging their employees to upload papers that have been accepted by a publisher of their choice to the institution's repository, as long as such mandates do not undermine the business model of the original publishers.

4.5 CONCLUSIONS

To conclude, a number of strategies are available to mitigate the social cost of a transition to OA academic publishing. At present, it seems advisable to proceed with both the green and the gold road to open access. An exclusive transition to gold OA might merely result in the big publishers exploiting the universities on publication fees rather than on subscription

---

[22] Of course, the pivotal question is *why* the author is reluctant to publish the paper. From a social welfare point of view, it makes no sense to urge an author to publish her research results if she perceives them as preliminary and not ready for publication. This might be different if we imagine a situation where a scholar cooperates with a commercial institution and the latter wants to keep the results secret. But this is a different story and goes beyond the scope of this book.

fees, as is presently the case (Hagner 2015: 115). The option of secondary publication via the green road leaves the decision to switch to gold OA with the publishers and at the same time exerts some pressure on their subscription fees or publication fees, respectively. In the ideal case, this pressure should be strong enough to prevent serials prices from further dramatic increases without undermining commercial publishers' business model.[23] However, in the longer term

> the cost of processing journal submissions may fall to such a degree that a gold policy will not require high fees from authors. A move towards journals offering a pure certification service, rather than requiring multiple rounds of revision, will reduce journal costs (and the required publication fees) and lessen the time spent on writing referee reports (Armstrong 2015: F22).

This suggests that the future of academic publishing will most likely be characterized by an increasing importance of OA mega-journals with open post-publication reviews. Anyway, any successful policy towards the transition to OA has to make sure that only those articles are published that meet some minimum quality requirement and that reliable quality signals help potential readers find the best papers for their purpose. This is the most challenging demand on a beneficial transition to OA.

---

[23] One has to take into account that 'traditional subscription journals have an incentive to permit a degree of self-archiving ... This is because this helps to attract authors and also because wider readership will boost citations and impact factors, which in turn helps publishers market their journals to libraries' (Armstrong 2015: F8).

5. Summary and outlook

Digitization and the internet have dramatically changed the world (not only) of academic publishing. We have shown that the new technologies have not only triggered new ways of creating and disseminating scholarly articles, they also produce winners and losers, depending on the design of copyright law, the institutions and cultures of academic publishing, and the policies on academic publishing pursued by governments and other players.[1]

In chapters 1 and 2, we have shown that copyright protection allows traditional commercial publishers to establish a business model which enables them to make profits out of subscription fees. When discussing the transition to OA, we have to be aware that there are different approaches to copyright law in different regions of the world. In particular, a distinction must be made between the Anglo-American approach of 'copyright' and the continental European approach of 'authors' rights'.[2] The Anglo-American copyright is based on a utilitarian approach. Copyright is perceived as an instrument to promote authors' creativity for the benefit of the public domain and thereby to increase social welfare. By contrast, similarly to property rights in tangible goods, the continental European authors' rights are perceived as natural rights of the creators that comprise not only exploitation rights but also 'moral rights', including in particular the rights of *disclosure* (to determine when and how the work is released), of *attribution* (to be recognized as the creator of the work), and of *integrity* (protection of the work from changes unapproved by its author) (Baldwin 2014: 29–37). In a nutshell: 'Copyright encourages innovation and promotes dissemination. Authors' rights restrain distribution, inhibiting experimentation and public exposure. Authors' rights speak for creators, while copyright favors disseminators and interpreters and ultimately the audience' (Baldwin 2014: 15).

---

[1] For a more general view on how digital technology affects the adequacy of traditional doctrines, concepts and positive laws establishing intellectual property rights, such as copyright, patents, trademarks, designs and trade secrets, see Elkin-Koren and Salzberger (2013).

[2] See the excellent book by Baldwin (2014).

Whereas the 20th century saw some convergence of the Anglo-American model towards the continental European model, e.g. successive extensions of the duration of copyright protection, at the turn of the millennium, with the increasing role of digitization and the internet, the continental European approach of strengthening exclusive authors' rights has come under pressure.[3] As we have discussed in some detail in chapters 2 and 4, this applies in particular to academic publishing, where many initiatives have sought to weaken the exclusive rights of authors and publishers, who usually hold the copyright, and to facilitate access to research results.

From a broader perspective, one must take into account that access to scholarly information is important not only for a well-functioning academia, but also for economic and social development in general. There are two complementary explanations as to why the industrial revolution happened in Europe rather than elsewhere. One of them concerns the phenomena most famously described by Adam Smith, focusing on institutions such as well-defined and respected property rights, enforceable contracts and the rule of law.[4] The other one concerns precisely the access to scholarly information. It is most closely associated with Joseph Schumpeter and focuses on the generation and continuous improvement of new 'useful knowledge'. Mokyr (2017) has examined this second explanation in some detail, looking in particular at the period from 1500 to 1700, when a competitive 'market for ideas' (Coase 1974) first emerged. This development was facilitated by the political fragmentation of Europe, which made it easy for scholars to settle elsewhere if their work was not compatible with the ruling ideology in their home country. Under those conditions, a transnational community of the preeminent thinkers of the time had developed, including, for example, European scholars from the west (Erasmus of Rotterdam, Hugo Grotius, René Descartes), the centre (Paracelsus, Johannes Kepler, Gottfried Wilhelm Leibniz), the north (Tycho Brahe, Francis Bacon, Isaac Newton), the south (Galileo Galilei, Giordano Bruno), and the east of Europe (Marin Getaldić, Jan Brozek), a community that became known as the 'Republic of Letters': 'The main rules governing the Republic of Letters were freedom of entry, contestability, that is, the right to challenge any form of knowledge, transnationality, and a commitment to placing new knowledge in the public domain' (Mokyr 2017: 189). The Republic was governed not by market

---

[3] On the, at times, fierce discussions among the relevant players in Germany, see Eger (2015).

[4] See, for example, North and Thomas (1973), North (1981, 1990) and Acemoglu and Robinson (2012).

prices but by another 'currency' – the priority rule, which attributes success to the person whom the scientific community recognizes as being the
first to make an original contribution (Merton 1957, 1973; Osterloh and
Frey 2014: 79). Scholars originally disseminated research results via the
circulation of handwritten letters and the exchange of published papers
and pamphlets over great distances, they also travelled to foreign universities for personal visits or study periods, or to relocate to an intellectual
climate that is more amenable to their research.[5] In the mid-17th century,
the exchange was institutionalized with the establishment of permanent
literary and scientific academies and the first scholarly journals in England
and France.[6] The availability of movable type printing, already invented
in the mid-15th century by Gutenberg, and Latin as the original lingua
franca facilitated the dissemination of scholarly information among the
members of the Republic. By the late 17th century, more and more works
were published in vernacular languages, were circulated across Europe
to a broader public, and, in the following centuries, ultimately served as
informational inputs to the industrial revolution.[7]

Today, with digitization and the internet, open access to academic
publishing could help to create a modern 'Republic of Letters', say a
'Republic of Bits and Bytes', supplying society with important scholarly
information. This would require some collective action to ensure that
high-quality scholarly information is generated based on the researcher's
curiosity and effectively disseminated to users at reasonable (search) cost.
Any such system must take into account the specific interests and incentives of a range of different actors, including authors, academic libraries,
learned societies, for-profit and non-for-profit publishers and individual
readers of scholarly articles, but also governments, research sponsors and
the tax-paying public. Economists know that 'there ain't no such thing as
a free lunch' – somebody has to pay for the creation and dissemination of
academic works. They also know that every method of allocating the cost
of creating and disseminating scholarly works to specific players affects
those players' incentives and thereby the provision of scholarly information to society in specific and predictable ways.

We have seen that the prevailing system of academic publishing, which
in most disciplines relies on the quality of publications in highly ranked
journals, not only helps readers in the ex-ante assessment of the value of

---

[5] For more details see Mokyr (2017: chapter 12).
[6] For additional information see Ramello (2010: 12–13).
[7] These developments also triggered the emergence of copyright law. See
Eger and Scheufen (2012).

an article but also creates systematic biases in the selection of articles for publication. In conjunction with public peer review and the calculation of reliable individual impact factors, open access may allow (academic) readers to select articles that are better suited to their own research intention, and it may also reduce bias in publication by reducing the incentive for 'slicing' and similar strategies that only promote the author's reputation but fail to create visible added value for the academic community and beyond. In general, the global spread of information technology has dramatically reduced the cost of editing and disseminating scholarly articles, which reinforces the case for OA. However, OA as such is not a panacea for a solution to all these problems; as always, the devil is in the detail. Let us summarize these details that were discussed at some length in previous chapters.

First, to the extent that OA journals are financed through article processing charges (APCs), there is always a risk of the quality of the published articles deteriorating (McCabe and Snyder 2005). This risk results, on the one hand, from the incentive of commercial publishers to increase the number of accepted articles by reducing their quality requirements below those that apply under the traditional business model. However, this risk evaporates if the perceived quality loss of a journal sufficiently reduces the APCs that the publisher can charge. On the other hand, the chance to earn APCs may attract predatory publishers who specialize in low-quality papers. Some collective action would be required to improve transparency and to warn inexperienced scholars. Non-for-profit initiatives to establish excellent new OA journals or to convert traditional journals into OA journals of high reputation should be supported by governments and research sponsors.[8] However, the difficulty is of course to give any such support to the initiatives with the highest value added for the academic community.

Second, a large-scale transition to open access may not solve the financial problems of the universities and research institutes and their academic libraries. APCs depend not only on the commercial publishers' costs but also on their bargaining power. As long as the big commercial publishers continue to own the most valuable journal titles, the negotiated APCs will remain high enough for the publishers to earn at least their present rate of return. One way to cope with this problem is to condition the eligibility for authors' APC subsidies on the publishers earning no more than a

---

[8] This holds only for pure OA journals but not for hybrid journals that enable publishers to engage in double dipping and price discrimination. See, for example Mueller-Langer and Watt (2016).

reasonable rate of return. However, since publication costs differ widely, any cap on APCs would have to be specific to individual disciplines and types of journals. The crucial problem is that this price regulation would not be feasible without establishing a regulatory bureaucracy with all the consequences we are familiar with, for example, from the regulation of natural monopolies (Baldwin et al. 2012).

Third, any APC subsidies or waivers raise the following trade-off: The stronger the financial support, the fewer excellent papers will fail to be published due to financial constraints on the part of the authors but, at the same time, the larger might be the risk that poor papers will be published, which is not only a direct waste of scarce resources but also makes it more difficult for the readers to select the most suitable articles.

Fourth, many learned societies own a few journals and use the profits from subscription fees to fund conferences, scholarships and so on. The effects of the transition to OA for the members depend on the details. If the transition boosts readership, additional advertising opportunities may yield new sources of income. However, if no additional income is forthcoming, the larger the share of readers who are not society members and the more APCs are subsidized out of membership fees, the more the members will suffer from the transition to OA.

> However, a principle of competition policy is that exploitative conduct cannot be justified by the use subsequently made of monopoly profits, however benign. In any case, if the activities of the association are valuable, it should be able to obtain funds directly from funding bodies rather than indirectly from libraries. It would be a pity if the special interests of associations were an impediment to widening access to research. (Armstrong 2015: F20)

Fifth, OA repositories complement OA journals by opening the content of subscription-based journals to some extent to the public. Adequate embargo periods should protect the business model of commercial publishers while still allowing the rapid dissemination of research results. Any regulation of embargo periods by law or by research sponsors should take into account that the average cited half-life of scholarly articles differs considerably across disciplines, which necessitates discipline-specific embargo periods.

Sixth and finally, a number of scholarly authors feel that OA mandates restrict their freedom of research, which suggests that such mandates must be applied with care, if at all. The more OA journals and repositories of high reputation exist, the less OA mandates are needed.

To conclude, we have shown that the gold road of open access financed by publication fees is to some extent the 'natural business model' for the publication of academic works. Why? On the one hand, academic works are non-rival goods. There is no good reason to deny non-payers access – except to create incentives for the provision of these goods. On the other hand, most authors of academic articles derive no direct material gain from their work. They seek to improve their reputation within the scientific community. Of course, somebody has to cover publishers' costs, but this can be done, in principle, by reallocating the existing funds from subscription fees to publication fees. So long as non-for-profit publishers, OA repositories or competition authorities exert sufficient downward pressure on publication fees there is no risk of the commercial publishers 'milking' the research sponsors. Thus, a well-designed system of OA journals will not destroy the authors' or the publishers' incentives to provide and disseminate academic articles.

Moreover, we have seen that a smart transition to OA – one that takes into account the different publication cultures in different disciplines, as well as the incentives faced by the relevant actors, including authors, commercial and non-commercial publishers, academic libraries, research sponsors, governments and taxpayers – has the potential to make academic publishing more efficient. The crucial point is to establish a reliable system of quality control for OA papers. This is not an easy task. However, we can rely on the experience of successful OA journals as best practice to facilitate access to research results for academic researchers and the broader public, to signal to (potential) authors the quality of the available journals and to reliably signal to the (potential) readers the quality of the published papers as perceived by the academic community. A well-designed system of OA publishing for academic articles should greatly reduce the social cost of the inefficient exclusion of non-payers without destroying the incentives to create high-quality academic works.

Appendix 1: The academic journal market

THE DATA

In analyzing the academic journal market, we have relied on three data sources: (1) Data on journals contained in the Journal Citation Report (JCR, 2014) from Thomson Reuter's Web of Science (WoS); (2) Data on journal prices from Bergstrom and McAffee (2013); (3) Metadata from the Directory of Open Access Journals (DOAJ) on all OA journals, following the definition of pure OA as outlined in the Budapest Open Access Initiative. All of these data sources were matched and adapted to create a data sample which yields information on all relevant aspects by publisher and by discipline. The process of creating the sample shall be explained briefly for a better understanding of the results presented in chapter 2. We will start with sources (1) and (2) as both are used to analyse the academic journal market in chapter 2.2. The sample we used for chapter 2.3 draws upon databases (1) and (3). We will explain data source (3) in Appendix 2 as it refers to the data creation of OA journals.

In chapter 2.2.1 we use data on journals contained in the JCR (2014) from WoS.[1] We match the regular JCR data with data on journals in particular disciplines and data on journals of particular publishers. First, the discipline-specific information is retrieved from WoS. For comparability with the metadata from the DOAJ, we retrieve only journals in disciplines that can unambiguously be assigned to the categorization of the Directory,[2] a criterion that led us to omit journals from 'Art and Architecture' and 'Philosophy and Religion'. In total, we extract 13 discipline-specific lists of journals, which we match with the JCR data using the journals' unique ISSN numbers. Each of the 13 lists is assigned a discipline dummy variable, and all journals not contained in any of the lists were assigned to the category 'other'. To identify the publishers, we

---

[1]   We cover both the Science Citation Index (SCI) and the Social Science Citation Index (SSCI) journals in WoS, with some overlap among the two lists.

[2]   For example, education and psychology are assigned to 'Social Science'. All medical fields are assigned to 'Health Science'.

use journal lists for the big five publishers: Elsevier, Springer, Taylor & Francis, Sage and Wiley-Blackwell. Again, we create dummy variables for each of these publishers, matching the JCR (2014) with each of the five journal lists via the journal ISSN number. For Elsevier, we find a list of 4,302 journals at 'Science Direct'. Journal lists for Springer (2,775 journals) and Wiley-Blackwell (1,509) were retrieved directly from the journal websites. For Sage (791) and Taylor & Francis (861), we retrieve the data from WoS by searching for the publisher names. Table A.2.1 provides an overview of the most important variables.

In chapter 2.2.2 we use a price database of internationally published academic journals compiled by Ted Bergstrom and Preston McAffee.[3] We only analyze journals for which a positive price is quoted both in 2004 and in 2013. Matching entries in both years were identified via ISSN numbers. In total, the database has information in both years for 4,398 journals, of which 4,080 have usable price data. Table A.2.2 provides an overview of the summary statistics of this database.

---

[3]   The data are available at http://journalprices.com/SummaryData.xls, with details and sources at http://journalprices.com/explanation2013.html.

Table A.2.1   *Summary statistics of JCR (2014), matched with disciplines and publisher lists*

Variable	Obs.	Mean	Std. Dev.	Min.	Max.
Journal Reputation Information					
IF	11,111	1.96	2.96	0	115.84
FiveIF	10,670	2.20	3.23	0	119.827
Eigenfactor	11,149	0.01	0.04	0	153.547
TotalCites	11,149	4,400.30	17,057.66	1	617,363
Journal Type Information					
SCI	11,149	0.77	0.42	0	1
SSCI	11,149	0.28	0.45	0	1
OA	11,149	0.08	0.27	0	1
Discipline Information					
Agri	11,149	0.02	0.15	0	1
Art	11,149	0.00	0.01	0	1
Bio	11,149	0.11	0.31	0	1
Bus	11,149	0.04	0.21	0	1
Chem	11,149	0.05	0.21	0	1
Earth	11,149	0.04	0.19	0	1
Health	11,149	0.13	0.33	0	1
Hist	11,149	0.02	0.12	0	1
LaPo	11,149	0.03	0.16	0	1
Lang	11,149	0.02	0.12	0	1
Math	11,149	0.06	0.23	0	1
Phil	11,149	0.00	0.00	0	1
Phys	11,149	0.04	0.20	0	1
Social	11,149	0.15	0.36	0	1
Tech	11,149	0.14	0.35	0	1
Other	11,149	0.33	0.47	0	1
Publisher Information					
Elsevier	11,149	0.16	0.37	0	1
Springer	11,149	0.11	0.32	0	1
Taylor & Francis	11,149	0.07	0.26	0	1
Sage	11,149	0.04	0.21	0	1
Wiley-Blackwell	11,149	0.10	0.30	0	1

*Table A.2.2   Summary statistics for the Bergstrom and McAfee (2013)
database*

Variable	Obs.	Mean	Std. Dev.	Min.	Max.
Discipline Information					
SMT	4080	0.29	0.45	0	1
HUMAN	4080	0.02	0.13	0	1
LIFE	4080	0.49	0.50	0	1
SOCIAL	4080	0.26	0.44	0	1
Journal Information					
AGE	4080	60.26	136.72	14	226
PROFIT	4080	0.64	0.48	0	1
Price Information					
Price per Article (2013)	4080	20.88	26.54	0.08	531.31
Price per Citation (2013)	4080	18.69	38.78	0.01	980.00
Price per Article (2004)	4080	14.68	17.42	0.06	360.09
Price per Citation (2004)	4080	12.84	46.98	0.00	1591.12
Composite Price Index (2004)	4080	11.95	20.73	0.04	754.26
Price Change (percent)	4080	72.13	178.48	−90.88	5740.00

JOURNALS IN DIFFERENT FIELDS OF RESEARCH

(a) Distribution of publishers by disciplines

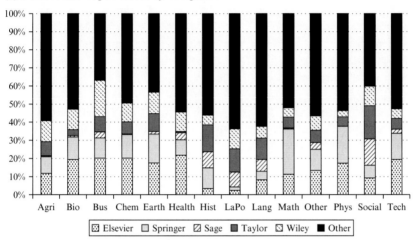

(b) Distribution of disciplines by publisher

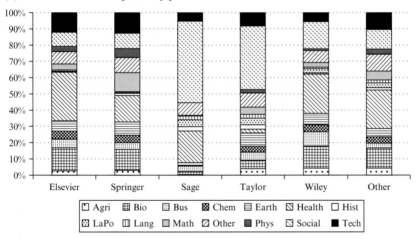

Source: Authors' calculations based on JCR (2014).

Figure A.2.1 Market shares in terms of number of journals by publishers and disciplines

Appendix 2: Open access journals

THE DOAJ DATA

In chapter 2.3.1 we use journal metadata from the DOAJ, which we extracted in May 2016. In total, we find 8,601 OA journals. Additional information is obtained by adapting our data in two respects. First, we create discipline dummies using the categorization applied by the DOAJ, which distinguishes the 15 fields enumerated in chapter 2, and we add a dummy 'other' to account for journals that cannot be assigned to any of these 15 fields. Note that some journals can be assigned to multiple fields, e.g. for interdisciplinary journals. In these cases we determine the discipline on the basis of the first level assignment to avoid counting journals twice. Moreover, a total of 3,208 journals were assigned to the discipline 'Science', with a more specific assignment on the second level. In each instance, we manually assigned the disciplines based on the assignment on the second level. For example, 'Science: Economics' was assigned to 'Bus' and 'Science: Microbiology' was assigned to 'Bio'. Second, using the journal ISSN, we matched the DOAJ metadata with the JCR (2014) database to add information on the impact factor (IF), the 'Five Year Impact Factor' (FiveIF), the Eigenfactor and normalized Eigenfactor. Table A.2.3 provides the summary statistics for the DOAJ database matched with JCR (2014).

Furthermore, we created a number of dummies to capture additional journal characteristics: *APC* indicates whether a journal charges article processing fees. Similarly, *submission fee* accounts for separate submission fees to be paid to the journal. *English* equals one if a journal is published in English, irrespective of any additional languages. *Review* indicates the presence of a review system, irrespective of its nature. Finally, *plagiarism* indicates whether a journal has some kind of rule on plagiarism. Note that we do not report the single discipline dummies above, but a variable field number which accounts for the number of a field from 1 = Agri to 15 = Tech and 16 = other. *WoS* is a dummy that is one if the respective journal is listed in the JCR (2014) and zero otherwise. We find that only 8.9 percent of all OA journals listed by the DOAJ are also listed in the JCR (2014).

Table A.2.3 *Summary statistics of DOAJ metadata, matched with JCR (2014)*

Variable	Obs.	Mean	Std. Dev.	Min.	Max.
Journal Characteristics					
APC	8,601	0.156	0.363	0	1
Submission Fee	8,601	0.007	0.082	0	1
English	8,601	0.713	0.452	0	1
Review	8,601	0.436	0.496	0	1
Plagiarism	8,601	0.284	0.451	0	1
Journal Information from JCR (2014)					
WoS	8,601	0.098	0.298	0	1
IF	703	1.592	1.747	0	19.250
FiveIF	703	1.594	1.898	0	21.111
Eigenfactor	703	0.006	0.021	0.00001	0.344
Eigenfactor, normalized	703	0.617	2.317	0	38.371

Source: Authors' calculations based on DOAJ metadata and JCR (2014).

OA JOURNALS IN DIFFERENT FIELDS OF RESEARCH

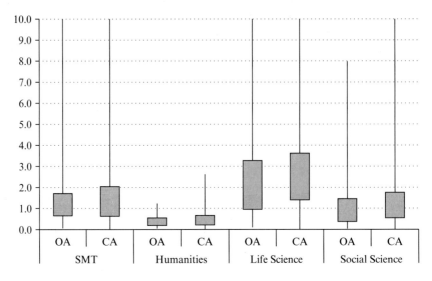

Source: Authors' evaluations using DOAJ metadata and JCR (2014).

Figure A.2.2   Boxplot of the IF (≤ 10) by research field: OA versus CA journals

Table A.2.4   Impact factor differences between OA and CA by research field

Field	Regime	Mean	N	Difference[*]
SMT	OA	1.62	182	0.18
	CA	1.8	2,706	
Humanities	OA	0.45	9	0.07
	CA	0.52	257	
Life science	OA	2.44	311	0.84***
	CA	3.28	2,341	
Social science	OA	1.06	103	0.33***
	CA	1.39	1,863	
Total	OA	1.93	605	0.2***
	CA	2.13	7,167	

Notes: * Difference in the mean IF between CA and OA journals. *** $p < 0.01$.

Source: Authors' calculations based on DOAJ metadata and JCR (2014).

Appendix 3: An international survey analysis

DESCRIPTIVE STATISTICS

Table A.3.1 Discipline averages of OA usage rates and degrees

Discipline	OA_pub	OA_degree	REP_pub	REP_degree
Agri	0.58	1.23	0.18	0.87
Art	0.42	0.80	0.28	1.10
Bio	0.66	1.82	0.16	0.75
Bus	0.35	0.67	0.40	1.36
Chem	0.38	0.84	0.14	0.59
Earth	0.54	1.18	0.18	0.81
Health	0.62	1.49	0.13	0.74
Hist	0.51	0.90	0.29	0.43
LaPo	0.45	0.84	0.36	1.18
Lang	0.46	0.88	0.29	1.13
Math	0.39	0.95	0.54	2.07
Phil	0.40	0.73	0.20	0.96
Phys	0.53	1.41	0.63	2.01
Social	0.53	1.13	0.30	1.32
Tech	0.40	0.92	0.25	1.13
Total	0.51	1.15	0.28	1.12

Table A.3.2   Discipline averages of OA relevance *and* OA awareness

Discipline	OA awareness	OA relevance
Agri	3.13	3.08
Art	3.24	2.85
Bio	3.62	3.39
Bus	2.85	2.28
Chem	2.87	2.23
Earth	3.33	3.00
Health	3.41	3.20
Hist	3.20	2.81
LaPo	3.11	2.48
Lang	3.15	2.67
Math	3.09	2.51
Phil	2.70	2.32
Phys	3.25	2.83
Social	3.27	2.76
Tech	3.08	2.56
Total	3.22	2.80

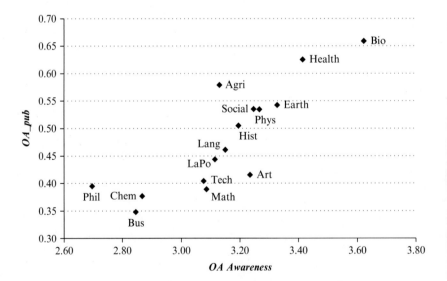

Figure A.3.1   Discipline averages of OA Awareness *and* OA_pub

EMPIRICAL RESULTS

Table A.3.3 *Culture averages for* no_monograph, refereed_j *and* j_ranking

Culture	*no_monograph*	*refereed_j*	*j_ranking*
green	2.052	3.781	3.554
gold	2.047	3.809	3.595
gray	2.677	3.594	3.363

Table A.3.4 Gold road regression results for the interaction with the green OA culture, 'Physics and Astronomy' excluded

Variables	(1)	(2)	(3)	(4)	(5)	(6)
years_acad	0.00385	0.00358	0.0117	0.00403	0.00385	0.00354
	(0.00486)	(0.00489)	(0.0172)	(0.00497)	(0.00495)	(0.00493)
years_acad2			-0.000182			
			(0.000384)			
professional	0.791***	0.792***	0.758***	0.736***	0.735***	0.734***
	(0.195)	(0.195)	(0.206)	(0.195)	(0.195)	(0.195)
institute		-0.214	-0.211	-0.244	-0.244	-0.243
		(0.172)	(0.172)	(0.172)	(0.172)	(0.172)
no_publication	-0.169**	-0.168**	-0.167**	-0.165**	-0.166**	-0.169**
	(0.0669)	(0.0669)	(0.0669)	(0.0665)	(0.0666)	(0.0667)
no_monograph	-0.219***	-0.224***	-0.224***	-0.226***	-0.227***	-0.225***
	(0.0465)	(0.0469)	(0.0469)	(0.0470)	(0.0468)	(0.0467)
refereed_j	0.0310	0.0358	0.0358	0.0301	0.0311	0.0323
	(0.0888)	(0.0889)	(0.0889)	(0.0893)	(0.0894)	(0.0893)
j_ranking	0.299***	0.297***	0.297***	0.287***	0.285***	0.283***
	(0.0694)	(0.0694)	(0.0694)	(0.0695)	(0.0694)	(0.0695)
oa_importance	0.0349	0.0354	0.0357			
	(0.0430)	(0.0429)	(0.0430)			
oa_quality	-0.0451	-0.0430	-0.0435			
	(0.0375)	(0.0377)	(0.0378)			
oa_future	0.0672	0.0671	0.0669	0.0396		
	(0.0462)	(0.0461)	(0.0461)	(0.0445)		

	(1)	(2)	(3)	(4)	(5)	(6)
oa_readership	0.0471	0.0474	0.0475	0.0499	0.0617	
	(0.0500)	(0.0499)	(0.0499)	(0.0489)	(0.0474)	
oa_citation	0.0470	0.0467	0.0469	0.0461	0.0499	0.0907***
	(0.0433)	(0.0432)	(0.0432)	(0.0425)	(0.0426)	(0.0312)
awareness				0.231***	0.236***	0.237***
				(0.0480)	(0.0477)	(0.0478)
relevance				−0.160***	−0.157***	−0.152***
				(0.0454)	(0.0454)	(0.0451)
west	0.314	0.334	0.330	0.413	0.417	0.439
	(0.335)	(0.336)	(0.335)	(0.336)	(0.336)	(0.336)
east	0.679*	0.696*	0.695*	0.848**	0.841**	0.863**
	(0.357)	(0.358)	(0.358)	(0.360)	(0.360)	(0.359)
emerg	0.487	0.499	0.496	0.649*	0.634*	0.639*
	(0.360)	(0.360)	(0.359)	(0.361)	(0.361)	(0.361)
south	0.626*	0.630*	0.624*	0.703**	0.702**	0.725**
	(0.338)	(0.338)	(0.337)	(0.339)	(0.339)	(0.339)
Observations	9,821	9,821	9,821	9,821	9,821	9,821
Pseudo R^2	0.028	0.029	0.029	0.035	0.035	0.034

Notes: Robust standard errors in parentheses. Constant not reported. *** p<0.01, ** p<0.05, * p<0.1.

Table A.3.5   Green road regression results for the interaction with the green OA culture, 'Physics and Astronomy' excluded

Variables	(1)	(2)	(3)	(4)
years_acad	−0.00803*	−0.00476	−0.0265*	−0.00494
	(0.00447)	(0.00474)	(0.0144)	(0.00492)
years_acad2			0.000495	
			(0.000315)	
professional	1.179***	1.237***	1.320***	1.229***
	(0.179)	(0.182)	(0.184)	(0.183)
institute		−0.0849	−0.0909	−0.0709
		(0.149)	(0.149)	(0.151)
no_publication	−0.308***	−0.181***	−0.182***	−0.173**
	(0.0592)	(0.0652)	(0.0652)	(0.0675)
no_monograph	−0.222***	−0.401***	−0.402***	−0.394***
	(0.0412)	(0.0478)	(0.0477)	(0.0487)
refereed_j	0.136	0.184	0.185	0.150
	(0.0997)	(0.112)	(0.112)	(0.110)
j_ranking	0.475***	0.494***	0.495***	0.473***
	(0.0714)	(0.0784)	(0.0784)	(0.0786)
rep_importance		−0.00260	−0.00396	0.0201
		(0.0472)	(0.0471)	(0.0490)
rep_readership		0.516***	0.518***	0.506***
		(0.0622)	(0.0621)	(0.0626)
rep_citation		−0.177***	−0.179***	−0.170***
		(0.0473)	(0.0474)	(0.0477)
rep_quality		0.585***	0.586***	0.579***
		(0.0386)	(0.0386)	(0.0386)
west				0.302
				(0.275)
east				−0.196
				(0.323)
trans				−0.0651
				(0.319)
south				0.456*
				(0.277)
Observations	9,821	9,821	9,821	9,821
Pseudo R^2	0.038	0.191	0.192	0.196

Notes: Robust standard errors in parentheses. Constant not reported. *** $p<0.01$, ** $p<0.05$, * $p<0.1$.

Appendix 4: The questionnaire

PART A: PERSONAL QUESTIONS

A.1. Which of the following disciplines best describes your profession? (dummy choices, vertical rating[1])
Agriculture and Forestry
Arts and Architecture
Biology and Life Science
Business and Economics
Chemistry
Earth and Environmental Sciences
Health Sciences
History and Archaeology
Languages and Literature
Law and Political Sciences
Mathematics and Statistics
Philosophy and Religion
Physics and Astronomy
Social Sciences
Technology and Engineering
Other (input field)[2]

A.2. What is your nationality? (dummy choices, vertical rating)
Afghanistan
Albania
. . .

A.3. What is your gender? (dummy choices, vertical rating)
Male
Female

---

[1]   Vertical rating means that respondents were able to choose only one of the answer choices.
[2]   Please note that all 'other' fields of research were manually categorized according to the DOAJ categories.

A.4. Profession (input field)
What is your age?
Years spent in academia?

A.5. What is your academic position? (dummy choices, vertical rating)
Professor (tenured)
Professor (non-tenured)
Postdoc (tenured)
Postdoc (non-tenured)
PhD student
Other (input field)

A.6. Are you a member of a professional association?
If so, please specify the most important one (input field)

A.7. How important do you consider the following criteria to be for your academic career? (0 to 5 rating for each answer option)
Journal reputation/ranking
Number of publications
Number of monographs
Teaching record
Acquisition of third party funds
International experience
Is there any other aspect you consider important? If so, which one? (input field)

A.8. How important do you consider the following venues of publication to be in your discipline? Contributions to. . . (0 to 5 rating)
Refereed journal
Non-refereed journal
Conference volume
Yearbook
Liber amicorum (Festschrift)
Blogs
Other books
Is there any other venue you consider important? If so, which one? (input field)

PART B1: GOLD ROAD OF OA (i.e. OA JOURNALS)

B1. Intro:

In the following, a journal is considered to provide general services like *peer-review*, editorial and typesetting tasks. An 'Open Access' Journal is a journal that allows any reader to read, download, copy, distribute, print, search, or link to the full texts of these articles without any financial or other barrier but internet access. A 'Closed Access' Journal is considered to not fully satisfy these requirements of a pure 'Open Access' journal, i.e. access to these journals is not free but restricted to individual and/or institutional subscription.

B.1. Please express your opinion on the following issues. (0 to 5 rating)

How aware are you of the concept of 'Open Access Journals'? How would you categorize your experience with this concept?
How would you assess the standing of 'Open Access Journals' in your discipline?

B.2. Have you ever published a paper in an 'Open Access' journal? (dummy choices, vertical rating)

Yes[3]
No[4]

B.3. Have you ever published any academic works during your career in academia? (dummy choices, vertical rating)

Yes
No

B.4. I have not yet used 'Open Access Journals' as a possible publishing outlet because. . . (0 to 5 rating)

I'm not willing to pay author fees for publishing my works in a journal.
It is rather uncommon in my discipline to publish in 'Open Access Journals'.
In my discipline, the classical 'Closed Access Journals' have a higher standing than 'Open Access Journals'.

---

[3] 'Yes' takes the respondent to questions B.6–B.12.
[4] 'No' takes the respondent to questions B.3–B.5.

B.5. I would be willing to publish my works in 'Open Access Journals' in the future if. . . (0 to 5 rating)

Author fees were zero or reasonable.
Other colleagues in my discipline also published their works in 'Open Access Journals'.
'Open Access Journals' achieved a better standing in my discipline.

B.6. What percentage of your journal publications *of the last five years* are published in 'Open Access' journals? (choices: < 10%, 10–25%, 25–50%, 50–75%, >75%)

B.7. Have you ever paid any 'author fees' for publishing a paper in an 'Open Access Journal'? (0/1)

B.8. Did you ever abstain from publishing a paper in an 'Open Access Journal' because you could not afford the author fees? (rating: never, seldom, sometimes, often, very often)

B.9. Would you generally be willing to pay the author fee out of your own pocket? (0/1)

B.10. Who did usually pay the author fees? (dummy choices, vertical rating)

Faculty
University
Third-Party Funds
Me

B.11. Can you name three 'Open Access Journals' that play an important role in your discipline? (input field)

B.12. Have you ever used the 'Open Choice' option? (0/1)

PART B2: RATING OF OA JOURNALS[5]

B2. Intro:

---

5   Part B2 is answered by all respondents.

Imagine you have to decide whether to publish your paper in an 'Open Access Journal' or a 'Closed Access Journal'.

B.13. Please indicate whether you agree or disagree with the following statements. (0 to 5 rating)

In my discipline, 'Open Access Journals' are considered to be more important than 'Closed Access Journals'.
I personally think that contributions to 'Open Access Journals' are at least as good in quality as contributions to 'Closed Access Journals'.
I personally think that authors of high reputation will prefer to publish their articles in 'Closed Access Journals'.
I personally think that young researchers are reluctant to publish their articles in 'Open Access Journals'.
I personally think that in my discipline, 'Open Access Journals' should play a larger role in the future.

B.14. Comparing 'Open Access Journals' to 'Closed Access Journals', I think. . . (0 to 5 rating)

'Open Access Journals' attract wider readership for my works.
'Open Access Journals' increase my citations.
'Open Access Journals' are more widely disseminated and increase the visibility of my works.

PART C1: THE GREEN ROAD (OA REPOSITORIES)

C1. Intro:

A repository or archive is a platform to provide free and unrestricted access to academic papers via the internet. In contrast to journal publishing, this form of publication does not involve any peer-review or other services but only requires the contributions to be of 'academic character'. Examples of such archives are 'arXiv.org' or 'SSRN'.

C.1. Have you ever deposited a work at a repository or archive? (dummy choices, vertical rating)

Yes[6]

---

[6] 'Yes' takes the respondent to questions C.4–C.8.

No[7]

C.2. Please confirm again that you have not deposited any of your works on self-archiving platforms or other websites. (dummy choices, vertical rating)

Yes, I have not provided free access to my works via the internet.
No, I do have academic works which can be downloaded for free via the internet. However, I'm using other platforms but repositories. (0/1)

C.3. I have not yet deposited any of my works on a repository, because. . . (0 to 5 rating)

This would reduce my chance of getting the paper published in a journal.
The usage of repositories is not well respected in my discipline.
I was not aware of the possibility to deposit my works on such repositories.

C.4. Where do you typically self-archive your works? (input field)

C.5. What percentage of your papers published *in the last five years* are available on self-archiving platforms? (Choices, <10%, 10–25%, 25–50%, 50–75%, >75%)

C.6. In my experience. . . (0 to 5 rating)

Self-archiving reduces the chance of getting my paper published in a journal afterwards (0 to 5 rating)
Researchers are rather reluctant to deposit their works on a repository to increase the chance to be accepted in a journal. (0 to 5 rating)

C.7. Have you ever run into a conflict with your publisher due to self-archiving of a published paper? (choices: no, sometimes, often, very often)

C.8. Should legislation award authors an inalienable right of secondary publication? (dummy choices, vertical rating)

No, secondary publication rights should be freely negotiated between authors and publishers.
Yes, legislation should award the author an inalienable right of secondary publication no later than 12 months after primary publication.

---

[7] 'No' takes the respondent to questions C.2–C.3.

Yes, legislation should award the author an inalienable right of secondary publication more than 12 months after primary publication.
I don't know.

PART C2: RATING OF OA REPOSITORIES[8]

C2. Intro:

Imagine you have to decide whether to deposit your most recent paper on a repository.

C.9. Please indicate whether you agree or disagree with the following statements. (0 to 5 rating)

In my field, self-archiving is more important than publishing in refereed journals.
I primarily use repositories/archives as a source for finding new research literature.

C.10. I think self-archiving can. . . (0 to 5 rating)

Increase the readership of my works.
Improve the visibility of my works.

C.11. I think self-archiving endangers the economic survival of academic publishers. (0 to 5 rating)

C.12. How do you generally assess the quality of papers deposited on repositories in your field? (0 to 5 rating)

---

[8]   Part C2 was answered by all respondents.

References

Acemoglu, D. and J. Robinson (2012), *Why Nations Fail: The Origins of Power, Prosperity, and Poverty*, New York, NY: Crown.

Agrawal, A.A. (2014), 'Four More Reasons to be Skeptical of Open-Access Publishing', *Trends in Plant Science*, 19 (3), 133.

Anderson, R. (2015), 'Should We Retire the Term "Predatory Publishing"?', *The Scholarly Kitchen*, May 11, accessed 9 February 2017 at https://scholarlykitchen.sspnet.org/2015/05/11/should-we-retire-the-term-predatory-publishing/.

Archambault, E., D. Amyot, D. Campbell, J. Caruso, P. Deschamps, A. Nicole, F. Provencher, L. Rebout and G. Roberge (2014), *Evolution of Open Access Policies and Availability, 1996–2013*, accessed 3 November 2016 at http://science-metrix.com/files/science-metrix/publications/d_4.5_sm_ec_dg-rtd_oa_policies_proportion_oa_1996-2013_v05p_0.pdf.

Armstrong, M. (2015), 'Opening Access to Research', *Economic Journal*, 125 (586), F1–F30.

Awre, C. (2006), 'The Technology of Open Access', in N. Jacobs (ed.), *Open Access: Key Strategic, Technical and Economic Aspects*, Oxford, UK: Chandos Publishing, pp. 55–62.

Baker, M. (2016), 'Open-access Index Delists Thousands of Journals. Many Publications Did Not Reapply after Leading Directory Tightened Its Quality Criteria', *Nature*, 533, doi:10.1038/nature.2016.19871.

Baldwin, P. (2014), *The Copyright Wars. Three Centuries of Trans-Atlantic Battle*, Oxford, UK and Princeton, NJ: Princeton University Press.

Baldwin, R., M. Cave and M. Lodge (2012), *Understanding Regulation. Theory, Strategy, and Practice*, Second Edition, Oxford, UK and New York, NY: Oxford University Press.

Beall, J. (2013), 'The Open-Access Movement Is Not Really about Open Access', *tripleC*, 11 (2), 589–97, accessed 9 February 2017 at http://www.triple-c.at/index.php/tripleC/article/viewFile/525/514.

Bénabou, R. and J. Tirole (2003), 'Intrinsic and Extrinsic Motivation', *Review of Economic Studies*, 70, 489–520.

Bergstrom, Th.C. (2013), http://www.journalprices.com/, accessed 25 September 2017.

Bergstrom, Th.C., P.N. Courant, R.P. McAfee and M.A. Williams (2014), 'Evaluating Big Deal Journal Bundles', *Proceedings of the National Academy of Sciences of the United States of America (PNAS)*, 111 (26), 9425–30.

Bergstrom, Th.C. and R.P. McAffee (2013), 'Big Deal Contract Project', accessed 31 May 2017 at http://econ.ucsb.edu/~tedb/Journals/BundleCon tracts.html.

Bergstrom, Th.C. and D.L. Rubinfeld (2010), 'Alternative Economic Designs for Academic Publishing', in R.C. Dreyfuss, H. First and D.L. Zimmerman (eds), *Working Within the Boundaries of Intellectual Property. Innovation Policy for the Knowledge Society*, Oxford, UK and New York, NY: Oxford University Press, pp. 137–48.

Bhattacharjee, Y. (2011), 'Saudi Universities Offer Cash in Exchange for Academic Prestige', *Science*, 334 (6061), 1344–5.

Björk, B.-C. (2016), 'The Open Access Movement at a Crossroads – Are the Big Publishers and Academic Media Taking Over?', *Learned Publishing*, 29 (2), 131–4.

Björk, B.-C. (2013), 'Open Access Subject Repositories – an Overview', preprint of an article accepted for publication in the Journal of the American Society for Information Science and Technology, accessed 6 November 2016 at http://www.openaccesspublishing.org/repositories/ Subject_Repositories.pdf.

Björk, B.-C., P. Welling, M. Laakso, P. Majlender, T. Hedlund and G. Gudnason (2010), 'Open Access to the Scientific Journal Literature: Situation 2009', *PLoS ONE* 5 (6), e11273. doi:10.1371/journal. pone.0011273.

Bornmann, L. and R. Mutz (2015), 'Growth Rates of Modern Science: A Bibliometric Analysis Based on the Number of Publications and Cited References', *Journal of the Association for Information Science and Technology*, 66 (11), 2215–22.

Coase, R. (1974), 'The Market for Goods and the Market for Ideas', *American Economic Review*, 64 (2), 384–91.

Coccia, M. (2006), 'Economic and Social Studies of Scientific Research: Nature and Origins', *Working Paper CERIS-CNR*, 8 (7).

Dasgupta, P. and J. David (1987), 'Information Disclosure and the Economics of Science and Technology', in G.R. Feiwel (ed.), *Arrow and the Ascent of Modern Economic Theory*, London, UK: Macmillan Press.

Diamond, A.M. (2005), 'Measurement, Incentives and Constraints in Stigler's Economics of Science', *The European Journal of the History of Economic Thought*, 12 (4), 635–61.

Eckdahl, T. (2004), 'Review of: PLoS Biology – A Freely Available, Open Access Online Journal', *Cell Biology Education*, 3 (1), 15–17.

Edlin, A.S. and D.L. Rubinfeld (2005), 'The Bundling of Academic Journals', *American Economic Review – Papers and Proceedings*, 95 (2), 441–5.

Edlin, A.S. and D.L. Rubinfeld (2004), 'Exclusion or Efficient Pricing? The "Big Deal" Bundling of Academic Journals', *Antitrust Law Journal*, 72 (1), 119–57.

Eger, T. (2015), 'Copyright Under Fire: Some Comments from a Law and Economics Perspective on the Heated Debate on Copyright Law', *Hamburg Law Review*, 1 (2), 25–40.

Eger, T., M. Kraft and P. Weise (1992), 'On the Equilibrium Proportion of Innovation and Imitation', *Economics Letters*, 38, 93–7.

Eger, T. and M. Scheufen (2012), 'The Past and the Future of Copyright Law: Technological Change and Beyond', in J. De Mot (ed.), *Liber Amicorum Boudewijn Bouckaert*, Brugge: die Keure, pp. 37–64.

Eger, T., M. Scheufen and D. Meierrieks (2016), 'The Determinants of Open Access Publishing: Survey Evidence from Countries in the Mediterranean Open Access Network (MedOANet)', *Economia e Politica Industriale*, 2 (7), 1–27, online: DOI: 10.1007/s40812-016-0027-8.

Eger, T., M. Scheufen and D. Meierrieks (2015), 'The Determinants of Open Access Publishing: Survey Evidence from Germany', *European Journal of Law and Economics*, 39 (3), 475–503, online: DOI: 10.1007/s10657-015-9488-x.

Elkin-Koren, N. and E.M. Salzberger (2013), *The Law and Economics of Intellectual Property in the Digital Age. The Limits of Analysis*, London, UK and New York, NY: Routledge.

Eve, M.P. (2014), *Open Access and the Humanities. Contexts, Controversies and the Future*, Cambridge, UK: Cambridge University Press.

Feess, E. and M. Scheufen (2016), 'Academic Copyright in the Publishing Game: a Contest Perspective', *European Journal of Law and Economics*, 42 (2), 263–94.

Flexner, A. (1938/2017), 'The Usefulness of Useful Knowledge', originally published in *Harper's Magazine* (1939); republished by Princeton University Press, with a companion essay by R. Dijkgraaf.

Frey, B.S. (1997), *Not Just for the Money. An Economic Theory of Personal Motivation*, Cheltenham, UK and Northampton, MA: Edward Elgar Publishing.

Frey, B.S. and M. Osterloh (2015), 'Impact Faktoren. Absurde Vermessung der Wissenschaft', *Soziale Welt*, 66 (2), 141–8.

Gans, J.S. and G.B. Shephard (1994), 'How Are the Mighty Fallen: Rejected Classic Articles by Leading Economists', *Journal of Economic Perspectives*, 8 (1), 165–79.

Garfield, E. (2005), 'The agony and the ecstasy – the history and meaning of the journal impact factor', paper presented at International

Congress on Peer Review and Biomedical Publication, Chicago, 16 September.

Garfield, E. (2003), 'The Meaning of the Impact Factor', *International Journal of Clinical and Health Psychology*, 3 (2), 363–9.

Garfield, E. (1955), 'Citation Indexes to Science: A New Dimension in Documentation through Association of Ideas', *Science*, 122 (3159), 108–11.

Gargouri, Y., V. Larivière, Y. Gingras, L. Carr, T. Brody and S. Harnad (2012), 'Green and Gold Open Access Percentages and Growth, by Discipline', in *17th International Conference on Science and Technology Indicators (STI), Science-Metrix and OST, Montreal, CA*, 285–92, accessed 7 February 2017 at http://eprints.soton.ac.uk/340294/.

Hagner, M. (2015), *Zur Sache des Buches*, Göttingen: Wallstein Verlag.

Harnad, S., T. Brody, F. Vallières, L. Carr, S. Hitchcock, Y. Gingras, C. Oppenheim, H. Stamerjohanns and E.R. Hilf (2004), 'The Access/Impact Problem and the Green and Gold Roads to Open Access', *Serials Review*, 30 (4), 310–14.

Hartgerink, C.H.J. (2017), *Publication Cycle: A Study of the Public Library of Science (PLOS)*, accessed 27 June 2017 at https://www.authorea.com/users/2013/articles/36067-publication-cycle-a-study-of-the-public-library-of-science-plos/_show_article.

Haucap, J., I. Loebert, G. Spindler and S. Thorwarth (2016), *Ökonomische Auswirkungen einer Bildungs- und Wissenschaftsschranke im Urheberrecht*, DICE Ordnungspolitische Perspektiven, No. 86, Düsseldorf: Düsseldorf University Press, accessed 11 April 2017 at http://www.dice.hhu.de/fileadm in/redaktion/Fakultaeten/Wirtschaftswissenschaftliche_Fakultaet/DICE/ Ordnungspolitische_Perspektiven/86_OP_Haucap_Loebert_Spindler_Th orwarth.pdf.

Haustein, S. and V. Larivière (2015), 'The Use of Bibliometrics for Assessing Research: Possibilities, Limitations, and Adverse Effects', in I. Welpe, J. Wollersheim, S. Ringelhan and M. Osterloh (eds), *Incentives and Performance – Governance of Research Organization*, Heidelberg: Springer, pp. 121–39.

Heller, M.A. (ed.) (2009), *Commons and Anticommons*, vol. I and II, Cheltenham, UK and Northampton, MA: Edward Elgar Publishing.

Heller, M.A. (1998), 'The Tragedy of the Anticommons: Property in the Transition from Marx to Markets', *Harvard Law Review*, 111 (3), 621–88.

Hirsch, J.E. (2005), 'An Index to Quantify an Individual's Scientific Research Output', *Proceedings of the National Academy of Sciences of the United States of America*, 102, 16569–72.

Houghton, J.W., B. Rasmussen, P. Sheehan, C. Oppenheim, A. Morris,

C. Creaser et al (2009), *Economic Implications of Alternative Scholarly Publishing Models: Exploring the Costs and Benefits*, A Report to the Joint Information Systems Committee, London and Bristol, accessed 1 February 2017 at https://www.researchgate.net/publication/48352211_Economic_implications_of_alternative_scholarly_publishing_models_exploring_the_costs_and_benefits_JISC_EI-ASPM_Project_A_report_to_the_Joint_Information_Systems_Committee_JISC.

Jahn, N. and M. Tullney (2016), 'A Study of Institutional Spending on Open Access Publication Fees in Germany', *PeerJ* 4:e2323; DOI 10.7717/peerj.2323.

Katz, M.L. (1984), 'Price Discrimination and Monopolistic Competition', *Econometrica*, 52 (6), 1453–71.

King, D.W. (2007), 'The Cost of Journal Publishing: a Literature Review and Commentary', *Learned Publishing*, 20 (2), 85–106.

Krujatz, S. (2012), *Open Access. Der offene Zugang zu wissenschaftlichen Informationen und die ökonomische Bedeutung urheberrechtlicher Ausschlussmacht für die wissenschaftliche Informationsversorgung*, Tübing en: Mohr Siebeck.

Laakso, M. and B.-C. Björk (2016), 'Hybrid Open Access – A Longitudinal Study', *Journal of Informetrics*, 10 (4), 919–32.

Landes, W.M. and R.A. Posner (2003), *The Economic Structure of Intellectual Property Law*, Cambridge, MA: Harvard University Press.

Larivière, V., S. Haustein and P. Mongeon (2015), 'The Oligopoly of Academic Publishers in the Digital Era', *PLoS ONE* 10 (6), accessed 6 November 2016 at http://journals.plos.org/plosone/article?id=10.1371/journal.pone.0127502.

Lawson, S. (2015), 'Fee Waivers for Open Access Journals', *Publications*, 3, 155–67.

Link, M. (2013), *Open Access im Wissenschaftsbereich*. Erlanger Schriften zum öffentlichen Recht, Bd. 4, Frankfurt/Main: Peter Lang.

Long, J.S. and J. Freese (2014), *Regression Models for Categorical Dependent Variables Using Stata*, 3rd edition, College Station, Texas: Stata Press.

Lozano, G.A., V. Larivière and Y. Gingras (2012), 'The Weakening Relationship Between the Impact Factor and Papers' Citations in the Digital Age', *Journal of the American Society for Information Science and Technology*, 63 (11), 2140–45.

McCabe, M.J. and C.M. Snyder (2015), 'Does Online Availability Increase Citations? Theory and Evidence from a Panel of Economics and Business Journals', *Review of Economics and Statistics*, 95 (2), 144–65.

McCabe, M.J. and C.M. Snyder (2005), 'Open Access and Academic Journal Quality', *American Economic Review*, 95 (2), 453–9.

Meho, L.I. (2007), 'The Rise and Rise of Citation Analysis', *Physics World*, 20 (1), 32–6.

Merton, R.K. (1973), 'The Sociology of Science', *Theoretical and Empirical Investigations*, Chicago, IL: The University of Chicago Press.

Merton, R.K. (1957), 'Priorities in Scientific Discovery: A Chapter in the Sociology of Science', *American Sociological Review*, 22 (6), 635–59.

Migheli, M. and G.B. Ramello (2014), 'Open Access Journals and Academics' Behavior', *Economic Inquiry*, 52 (4), 1250–66.

Migheli, M. and G.B. Ramello (2013), 'Open Access, Social Norms and Publication Choice', *European Journal of Law and Economics*, 35, 149–67.

Mittermaier, B. (2015), 'Double Dipping in Hybrid Open Access – Chimera or Reality?', accessed 3 November 2016 at https://juser.fz-juelich.de/record/190180/files/Double%20Dipping.pdf.

Mokyr, J. (2017), *A Culture of Growth. The Origins of the Modern Economy*, Oxford, UK and Princeton, NJ: Princeton University Press.

Moscon, V. (2014), *Open Access in Italy*, accessed 17 January 2017 at http://merlin.obs.coe.int/iris/2014/1/article32.en.html.

Mueller-Langer, F. and M. Scheufen (2013), 'Academic Publishing and Open Access', in R. Towse and Ch. Handke (eds), *Handbook on the Digital Creative Economy*, Cheltenham, UK and Northampton, MA: Edward Elgar Publishing, pp. 365–77.

Mueller-Langer, F., M. Scheufen and P. Waelbroeck (2016), Does Online Access Promote Research in Developing Countries? Empirical Evidence from Article-Level Data, Max Planck Institute for Innovation & Competition Research Paper No. 16-14.

Mueller-Langer, F. and R. Watt (2016), 'The Hybrid OA Citation Advantage: How Many More Cites is a $3,000 Fee Buying You?', Max Planck Institute for Innovation & Competition Research Paper No. 14-02.

Mueller-Langer, F. and R. Watt (2010), 'Copyright and Open Access for Academic Works', *Review of Economic Research on Copyright Issues*, 7 (1), 45–65, accessed 18 May 2017 at SSRN: https://ssrn.com/abstract=1647586.

Nelson, Ph. (1970), 'Information and Consumer Behavior', *Journal of Political Economy*, 78 (2), 311–29.

North, D.C. (1990), *Institutions, Institutional Change and Economic Performance*, Cambridge, UK: Cambridge University Press.

North, D.C. (1981), *Structure and Change in Economic History*, New York, NY: Norton.

North, D.C. and R.P. Thomas (1973), *The Rise of the Western World. A New Economic History*, Cambridge, UK: Cambridge University Press.

Osterloh, M. and B.S. Frey (2014a), 'Ranking Games', *Evaluation Review*, 39 (1), 102–29, accessed 8 April 2017 at https://www.bsfrey.ch/

articles/C_578_2014.pdf, 1–28.

Osterloh, M. and B.S. Frey (2014b), 'Academic Rankings between the "Republic of Science" and "New Public Management"', in A. Lanteri and J. Vromen (eds), *The Economics of Economists. Institutional Setting, Individual Incentives and Future Prospects*, Cambridge, UK: Cambridge University Press, pp. 77–103.

Pinfield, S. (2015), 'Making Open Access Work. The "State-of-the-Art" in Providing Open Access to Scholarly Literature', *Online Information Review*, 39 (5), 604–36, accessed 2 February 2017 at http://dx.doi.org/10.1108/OIR-05-2015-0167.

Powell, K. (2016), 'Does it Take Too Long to Publish Research?', *Nature*, 530 (7589), accessed 27 June 2017 at http://www.nature.com/news/does-it-take-too-long-to-publish-research-1.19320.

Prabha, Ch. (2007), 'Shifting from Print to Electronic Journals in ARL University Libraries', *Journal Serials Review*, 33 (1), 4–13, accessed 8 November 2016 at http://www.tandfonline.com/doi/abs/10.1080/00987913.2007.10765086.

Ramello, G.B. (2010), 'Copyright and Endogenous Market Structure: a Glimpse from the Journal-Publishing Market', *Review of Economic Research on Copyright Issues*, 7 (1), 7–29.

Regazzi, J.J. (2015), *Scholarly Communications. A History from Content as King to Content as Kingmaker*, Lanham, MD: Rowman & Littlefield.

Rochet, J.-C. and J. Tirole (2003), 'Platform Competition in Two-Sided Markets', *Journal of the European Economic Association*, 1 (4), 990–1029.

Ryan, R.M. and E.L. Deci (2000), 'Intrinsic and Extrinsic Motivations: Classic Definitions and New Directions', *Contemporary Educational Psychology*, 25, 54–67.

Samuelson, P.A. (1954), 'The Pure Theory of Public Expenditure', *Review of Economics and Statistics*, 36 (4), 387–9.

Schekman, R. (2013), *How to Break Free from the Stifling Grip of Luxury Journals*, accessed 8 February 2017 at http://theconversation.com/how-to-break-free-from-the-stifling-grip-of-luxury-journals-21669.

Scheufen, M. (2015), *Copyright Versus Open Access. On the Organisation and International Political Economy of Access to Scientific Knowledge*, Heidelberg: Springer.

Schimmer, R., K.K. Geschuhn and A. Vogler (2015), 'Disrupting the Subscription Journals' Business Model for the Necessary Large-scale Transformation to Open Access. A Max Planck Digital Library Open Access Policy White Paper', accessed 3 November 2016 at http://pubman.mpdl.mpg.de/pubman/item/escidoc:2148961:7/component/escidoc:2149096/MPDL_OA-Transition_White_Paper.pdf.

Schmidt, N. (2016), *Open Access. Hochschulrechtliche Veröffentlichungs-*

und urheberrechtliche Anbietungspflichten des Hochschulprofessors. Schriften zum geistigen Eigentum und zum Wettbewerbsrecht, Bd. 79, Baden-Baden: Nomos.

Seglen, P.O. (1997), 'Why the Impact Factor of Journals Should Not Be Used for Evaluating Research', *British Medical Journal*, 314 (7079), 498–502, accessed 8 November 2016 at http://www.bmj.com/content/314/7079/497.1.

Shavell, S. (2010), 'Should Copyright of Academic Works Be Abolished?', *Journal of Legal Analysis*, 2 (1), 301–58.

Siebeck, G. (2016), 'Die Urheber wurden gar nicht erst gefragt', *Frankfurter Allgemeine Zeitung*, 6 September, 14.

Solomon, D.J., M. Laakso and B.C. Björk; P. Suber (ed.) (2016), 'Converting Scholarly Journals to Open Access: A Review of Approaches and Experiences', *Copyright, Fair Use, Scholarly Communication, etc.*, Paper 27, accessed 11 May 2017 at http://digitalcommons.unl.edu/cgi/viewcontent.cgi?article=1026&context=scholcom.

Stephan, P.E. and S.S. Levin (1992), *Striking the Mother Lode in Science: The Importance of Age, Place and Time,* New York, NY: Oxford University Press.

STM Report (2015), *An Overview of Scientific and Scholarly Journal Publishing. Celebrating the 350th Anniversary of Journal Publishing,* published by the International Association of Scientific, Technical and Medical Publishers, The Hague, accessed 12 August 2017 at http://www.stm-assoc.org/2015_02_20_STM_Report_2015.pdf.

Suber, P. (2012), *Open Access*, Cambridge, MA: MIT Press.

Suber, P. (2006), 'Open Access in the USA', in N. Jacobs (ed.), *Open Access: Key Strategic, Technical and Economic Aspects*, Oxford, UK: Chandos, pp. 149–60.

Suber, P. and S. Arunachalam (2005), 'Open Access to Science in the Developing World', accessed 20 September 2017 at http://dash.harvard.edu/bitstream/handle/1/4725025/suber_worldinfocity.htm?sequence=1.

Tickel, A. (2016), *Open Access to Research Publications. Independent Advice,* accessed 17 January 2017 at www.gov.uk/government/uploads/system/uploads/attachment_data/file/499455/ind-16-3-open-access-report.pdf.

Van Noorden, R. (2014), 'Open-access Website Gets Tough. Leading Directory Tightens Listing Criteria to Weed Out Rogue Journals', *Nature*, 512, DOI: 10.1038/512017a.

Vogel, G. and K. Kupferschmidt (2017), 'Germany seeks "big flip" in publishing model', *Science*, 357 (6353), 744–5.

Wallace, F.H. and T.J. Perri (2016), *Economists Behaving Badly: Publications in Predatory Journals*, Appalachian State University, Department of

Economics Working Paper No. 16-08, accessed 18 May 2017 at http://econ.appstate.edu/RePEc/pdf/wp1608.pdf.

West, J.D., C.T. Bergstrom and Th.C. Bergstrom (2010), 'Bic Macs and Eigenfactor Scores: Don't Let the Correlation Coefficients Fool You', *Journal of the American Society for Information Science and Technology*, 61(9), 1800–807, available at http://works.bepress.com/ted_bergstrom/108/.

Willinsky, J. (2009), *The Access Principle. The Case for Open Access to Research and Scholarship*, Cambridge, MA: MIT Press.

Xia, J., J.L. Harmon, K.G. Connolly, R.M. Donnelly, M.R. Anderson and H.A. Howard (2015), 'Who Publishes in "Predatory" Journals?', *Journal of the Association for Information Science and Technology*, 66 (7), 1406–17.

Index